DORCHESTER
ABBEY

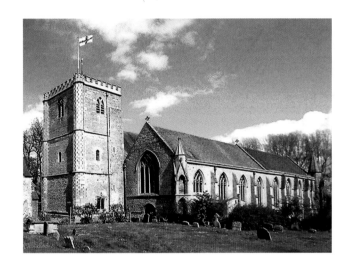

BERNIVS

This roundel of c.1250, the earliest stained glass in the abbey, shows St Birinus ('Bernius') being blessed by an enthroned archbishop, probably Asterius of Milan, who consecrated Birinus for the mission to Britain that brought him to Dorchester

THE DORCHESTER ABBEY PRESERVATION TRUST

DORCHESTER ABBEY

Church and People 635-2005

Edited by Kate Tiller

The Stonesfield Press

First published in Great Britain 2005
for The Dorchester Abbey Preservation Trust
by The Stonesfield Press
Peakes House, Stonesfield,
Witney, Oxon OX29 8PY

A CIP catalogue record for this book is available from the British Library

ISBN 0 9527126 4 4

Typeset in Monotype Bembo by The Stonesfield Press
Printed and bound in Great Britain by Information Press, Eynsham, Oxford

Contents

List of contributors

JAMES BOND is a freelance landscape archaeologist and former member of the Oxfordshire County Museum Service. He has a particular interest in monastic history and his book *Monastic Landscapes* was published in 2004. He is a Visiting Fellow in the Archaeology Department at the University of Bristol.

DR NICHOLAS DOGGETT is a historic buildings consultant and former conservation officer for South Oxfordshire. He has a long-standing interest in Dorchester Abbey, publishing an important article on the Saxon cathedral in 1986. He has subsequently researched the post-Dissolution reuse of monastic buildings.

NICHOLAS DUDLEY is a surgeon by profession. He lives in Dorchester and is active in the life of the abbey. He compiled a record of contemporary Dorchester to mark the millennium and has interviewed many local residents.

GRAHAM KEEVILL is a freelance archaeologist who has excavated a number of monastic sites. He directed the excavations at Dorchester Abbey in 2001, on which he has since published a detailed report.

DR KATE TILLER is Reader in English Local History (since 2004 Emerita) at Oxford University and a Fellow of Kellogg College. She has published and taught on the history of religion and community in England and on Oxfordshire history. She is a Visiting Fellow in English Local History at the University of Leicester.

DR GEOFFREY TYACK is an architectural historian, whose published works include *Oxford: an architectural guide* (1998). He has a particular interest in nineteenth-century building and restoration. He is Director of the Stanford University Centre in Oxford and a Fellow of Kellogg College.

Foreword

This book is a wonderful tribute to Dorchester Abbey and a precious gift to those who know, or will come to know, the building. As chairman of the Dorchester Abbey Campaign, I recognize and welcome it as a particularly valuable contribution to our work.

The purposes of the Campaign have been to undertake necessary repairs to the Abbey church, to make the building more useful and to enhance it as a place of worship.

Church repairs are always with us. The recent ones at Dorchester have been significant: most of the roofs and much of the flooring have been remade and the whole of the interior has been repaired and redecorated. The four medieval monuments and the tower clock have been conserved; the medieval wall-paintings are in course of conservation. And much else besides.

But the Campaign's ambition has been to bring about the conservative transformation of this great building so that it can be enjoyed much more, lift people's spirits and be better understood as one of the key sites in the development of Christianity in Britain.

So now the building is properly heated, it has a new, welcoming entrance and the disabled have been provided for. A permanent exhibition, designed to introduce visitors to the history of the Abbey and based on medieval stonework, has been set up in the new Cloister Gallery.

Development is going on in the tower to provide a better kitchen, a meeting room-cum-vestry and a storeroom.

The musical life of the Abbey has been enhanced by the gift of a piano and will be further enhanced by the reconfiguration of the organ.

Most important of all, the various points of focus for worship are being enriched: the Birinus Chapel, newly furnished and provided with the most beautiful altar cross and candlesticks; the chancel, for which new stalls are planned; and the shrine of St Birinus, which will be presented afresh as a reminder of the unity of all Christians.

The purpose of all this work has been to reinforce what Archbishop Robert Runcie saw as the special quality of Dorchester Abbey: 'a building which keeps alive the sense of the sacred in a busy world'.

This programme of works has been informed by history, and has even enabled scholars to understand it better. So it has been a pleasure for the Campaign to be associated with the publication of a new, and beautifully illustrated, history of the church and its people. We are grateful to all those who have contributed to it, and I particularly want to thank the most distinguished historian of Oxfordshire, Dr Kate Tiller, for devoting herself to this work, and the publisher of the book, Simon Haviland, whose gift to the Campaign has been its design and production.

Hugo Brunner

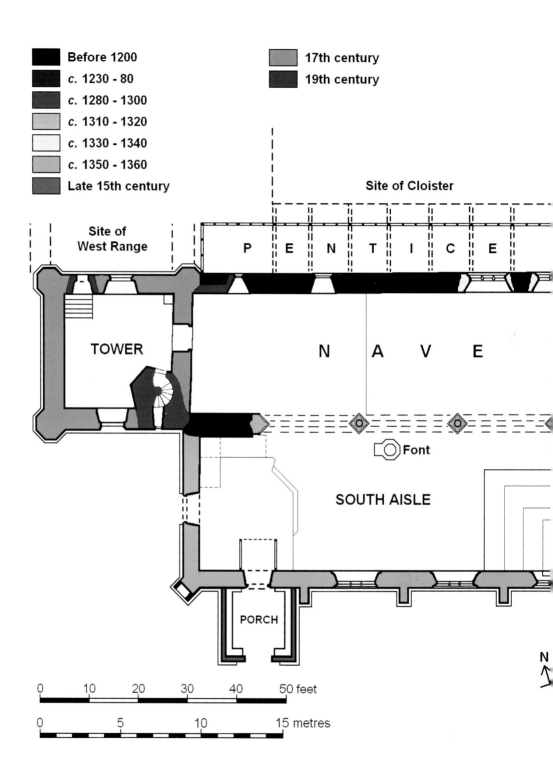

Before 1200

c. 1230 - 80

c. 1280 - 1300

c. 1310 - 1320

c. 1330 - 1340

c. 1350 - 1360

Late 15th century

17th century

19th century

Site of Cloister

Site of
West Range

P E N T I C E

TOWER

N A V E

Font

SOUTH AISLE

PORCH

N

0   10   20   30   40   50 feet

0   5   10   15 metres

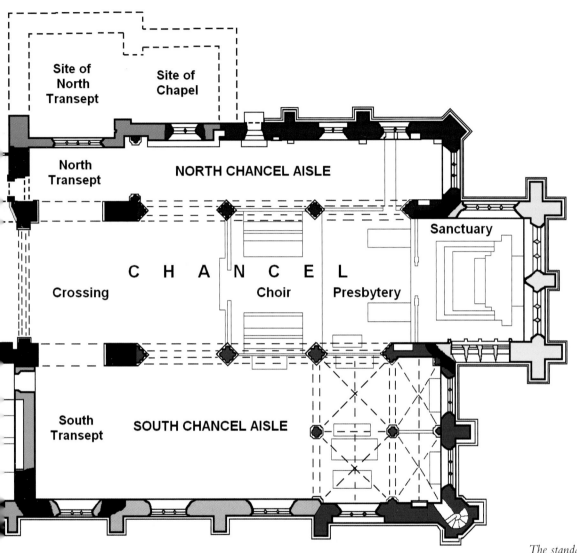

Site of
North
Transept

Site of
Chapel

North
Transept

NORTH CHANCEL AISLE

Sanctuary

Crossing

C H A N C E L

Choir

Presbytery

South
Transept

SOUTH CHANCEL AISLE

DORCHESTER ABBEY CHURCH

GROUND-PLAN

*The standard
names adopted
for the parts of
the abbey are
shown on this
ground-plan.
Various other
names have
been used at
different times
(see Chapter 8)*

Acknowledgements

Many skills and perspectives were needed to explore the history of Dorchester and its abbey. I am grateful to my fellow contributors to this book for bringing their diverse knowledge and insights to the project and to Hugo Brunner for first suggesting it. John Blair, Vincent Strudwick, Geoffrey Tyack and the Bishop of Dorchester have read and commented on parts of the text. I have benefited from helpful discussions with Malcolm Airs, Jerome Bertram and Adrienne Rosen. John Metcalfe, so much involved in the recent developments at the abbey, has been generous in his support; he and Warwick Rodwell have enabled me to draw on the recent major survey of the abbey site and fabric, completed only shortly before the publication of this book. Invaluable practical help has come from Tina and James Bond, in preparing maps and ground-plans; Phillipa Tarver in typing text; and Jenny Haviland in indexing. Simon Haviland has been a patient and thorough publisher as he encountered the sometimes surprising ways of historians. As ever, my husband Liam has lived with the project throughout, providing practical help and essential encouragement.

Illustrations play a key part in conveying the history of both building and people. I am happy to acknowledge the use of pictures from the following (figure numbers are given, unless otherwise indicated). Frank Blackwell, FRPS: half-title, frontispiece, 3, 9, 13, 15, 25, 26, 61, 72, p. 106, p. 124; The Bodleian Library, University of Oxford: 5, 7, 16, 21, 30, 33, 35; James Bond: 1, 17, 19, 20, ground-plans; Dorchester Historical Society and Dorchester Abbey Museum: 39, 43; Graham Keevill and Oxfordshire Architectural and Historical Society: 8; John Metcalfe: 71; Oxfordshire Photographic Archive, Oxfordshire County Council: 6, 29, 31, 42, 44-46, 49, 51, 54-59, p.107; Warwick Rodwell and Dorchester Parochial Church Council: 10, 11, 14, 18, 23, 24, 27; Kate Tiller: 50, 52, 62, chapter 8 I-VII; Liam Tiller: 22, 28, 34, 40, 41, p. 109, back cover.

Kate Tiller

Chapter One

Introduction

KATE TILLER

Dorchester is an exceptional place in many ways. It has been of central importance for human activity within the upper Thames valley over many millennia, and this is written into the fabric both of the town and its surroundings. The long history – and prehistory – of life, work, belief and death in the area is reflected in the remains of defended and open settlements, burial mounds, the strange religious monuments of earlier prehistory, and the Christian churches that are more familiar to us. Many of these sites survive only as buried archaeological remains, sometimes visible at ground level like the great Iron Age settlement at Dyke Hills, but more commonly invisible to the naked eye, unless exposed by archaeological fieldwork. Unfortunately the 'invisible' is all too often vulnerable to damage – even destruction – through accident like ploughing, or deliberate action such as quarrying and road-building. This has been the fate of many archaeological sites around Dorchester, though a great deal still survives. Fortunately, where above-ground archaeology is concerned, the town retains an impressive stock of historic buildings. These range from small-scale vernacular architecture to the grand and demonstrative. Dorchester Abbey falls firmly into the latter category, being known as one of the finest and most historically significant religious buildings, not only locally and regionally but also nationally.

Venerable and impressive buildings like Dorchester Abbey have always attracted high levels of interest on many fronts, from the local community (especially but not exclusively the parish) to national and international visitors. This attraction is deeply rooted in two distinct but interwoven strands: Christian worship and mission on the one hand, and the powerful draw of historic buildings and places on the other. The two strands come together in a particularly effective way at Dorchester, where the serenity of the centuries-old architecture can scarcely fail to inspire in the visitor some reflection on its

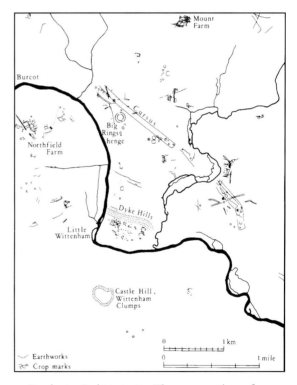

1. Dorchester: Prehistoric sites. The area near the confluence of the Thames and the Thame was an important focus of settlement, burial and ritual long before the coming of Christianity.

long history as a cathedral, abbey and parish church associated with many and varied spiritual journeys. It is little wonder that J. H. Parker, in his 1882 history of Dorchester, wrote of the abbey, town and surrounding landscape as 'a key to the history of England from the earliest period to the present time'.[1]

The length and richness of Dorchester's history also means that it is extremely complex. To unlock Parker's key involves unfolding many layers of sometimes imperfect or contradictory evidence, encountering major gaps along the way. For example, the medieval abbey's records have not survived, leaving us reliant on occasional references in other documents and intensive detective work on the surviving building. The building itself is multiphased and much changed, with none of the coherence lent by a single style, building period or designing hand. A succession of chroniclers (starting with William of Malmesbury in the 1120s), observers, antiquaries and (since the mid-nineteenth century) increasingly professional historians and archaeologists have trodden this path. Parker found that 'the architectural history of this magnificent church has been a battle-field of the archaeologists for the past half-century.'[2] This has not changed, and much further ink has been spilt and light cast since he wrote,[3] culminating in a recent upsurge of interest and investigation, using a range of modern techniques and associated with the restoration and development of the abbey around the millennium. This book is intended to capture and distil that increasing body of knowledge – and some of the remaining questions – about the abbey church and about its wider context and significance.

The following chronology provides a framework on which to base a more detailed picture:

Prehistory: Dorchester before Birinus

4,000–2,000 BC	Neolithic ritual complex: including the Cursus and Big Ring Henge.
2,000–1,100 BC	Bronze Age burials in round barrows: shields found in the Thames at Clifton Lock and Day's Lock.
Early Iron Age	Hill fort at Castle Hill, Wittenham Clumps.
Late Iron Age	Major settlement or *oppidum* at Dyke Hills.
1st century AD	Roman fort between Dyke Hills and area of the later town.
2nd century AD	Roman town developed in area of present settlement with earthen rampart and ditch of late second century.
3rd century AD	Wall built in front of town ramparts. Roman altar (found 1731); cremation burial (found in vicarage garden 1866).
410 AD	End of Roman rule but evidence of continuing occupation of Roman town at Dorchester.

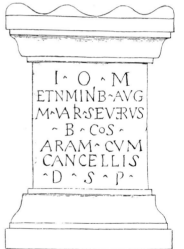

Jovi Optimo Maximo et numinibus Augusti Marcus Valerius Severus beneficiarius consulis aram cum cancellis de suo posuit

2. Altar dedicated to Jupiter by Marcus Varius Severus, who was a public official (beneficiarius consularis) in Dorchester in the early third century. It was discovered in 1731 and was later lost. (J. Horsley, 'Britannia Romana', 1732)

Early 5th century	Pagan burials of Germanic people.
5th–7th centuries	Saxon cemeteries, the largest at Wally's Corner.
5th–9th centuries	Excavated sites of Saxon buildings, showing sequence of fifth- to sixth-century sunken-floored huts (*grubenhäuser*), followed by seventh- and eighth-century rectangular timber-framed buildings, and finally dry-stone and cob structures. Buildings of the first two kinds uncovered on the abbey site in 2001 excavation.

Saxon Dorchester: Birinus and after

635	Birinus sent by Pope Honorius I to convert the Anglo-Saxons. Birinus baptizes Cynegils, King of Wessex, at Dorchester, with the Christian King Oswald of Northumbria standing sponsor. Cynegils and Oswald grant land at Dorchester for establishment of a bishopric. Birinus, the first bishop of the West Saxons, builds and dedicates several churches there.
*c.*650	Birinus died and buried at Dorchester.
660s	New Wessex see created at Winchester and cathedral built there.
670s	Dorchester briefly a Mercian see. Mercian bishoprics subsequently established at Leicester and Lindsey (in modern Lincolnshire), and Dorchester's episcopal status lapses.
*c.*690	Birinus's remains removed to Winchester and successive shrines built to him there.
870s	Dorchester a cathedral centre for the third time, refounded by Mercia when Viking-occupied Leicester became untenable. The diocese stretched from the Thames to the Humber.
*c.*1007	Foundation of county of Oxfordshire. Dorchester the centre of a hundred (including Dorchester, Chiselhampton, Clifton Hampden, Culham, Burcot, Drayton St Leonard, Stadhampton, South Stoke, Fifield (Benson), Epwell).

3. This early-fourteenth-century stained-glass panel in the east window is thought to show St Birinus preaching to King Cynegils of Wessex, whom he baptized at Dorchester in 635

3

PROTEGE BIRINE SINE FINE RAF RAS

4. *The fourteenth century was the heyday of the abbey, with extensive building and the development of the shrine to St Birinus. The tenor bell was a gift from Ralph Rastwold (d. 1383), lord of nearby Crowmarsh Gifford. It is inscribed PROTEGE BIRINE QUOS CONVOCO TU SINE FINE RAF RASTWOLD (Do thou, Birinus, protect for ever those whom I summon. Ralph Rastwold).*

1067	Death of Bishop Wulfwig, last Saxon Bishop of Dorchester. First Norman bishop, Remigius, styled Bishop of Dorchester, Leicester and Lincoln.
1072–3	See moved from Dorchester to Lincoln.

Medieval Dorchester: the Abbey

1072–*c*.1140	Dorchester a college of secular canons.
c.1125	William of Malmesbury described Dorchester and the 'beauty and state of its churches'.
c.1140	Dorchester refounded as an abbey by Bishop Alexander of Lincoln for the Arrouaisian branch of the Augustinian order.
1146 and 1163	Papal Bulls confirm abbey's possessions. Monks responsible for serving the parish, no vicarage being endowed.
c.1170	Lead font depicting the Apostles.
1224	Monks claimed to have discovered the body of St Birinus, and this is eventually recognized by Pope Honorius III.
c.1230–80	Extensions to north transept, subsequently developed into chancel aisle. Probable parallel development of south chancel aisle.
c.1280	Effigy of cross-legged knight (thought to be William de Valence the younger, died 1282).
1291	Taxation of Pope Nicholas IV recorded income of the abbey as £85 0s 2d.
1292 and 1293	Bishop Sutton of Lincoln granted an indulgence to all who visited Dorchester Abbey.
1301	Bishop Dalderby granted another indulgence of forty days to all who visited Birinus's bones.
c.1290–1300	Great rebuilding of the abbey in successive forms of Decorated gothic begins.

*c.*1310–1320	South chancel aisle added, two bays wide and housing new shrine to St Birinus.
*c.*1330–1340	Choir extended east by one bay. East window, Jesse window, south window, sedilia, stonework and glass.
14th century	West tower probably dates from this period; later rebuilt (1602).
*c.*1350–60	South aisle of nave built, enlarging the area available for parish worship and providing an ante-chapel to shrine.
*c.*1370–80	The two oldest bells, the seventh (dedicated to SS Peter and Paul) and the tenor (dedicated to St Birinus, in memory of Ralph Rastwold, who died in 1383).
1441, 1455, 1517, 1530	Visitations by the Bishops of Lincoln to the abbey revealing the state of monastic life at Dorchester.
1535	*Valor Ecclesiasticus* recorded income of abbey as £190 2s 4d.
1536	Dorchester Abbey dissolved.

Post-Dissolution: parish church, nonconformity and recusancy

1542	John Leland's description of Dorchester.
1544	Monastic buildings and precinct granted by the Crown to Sir Edmund Ashfield of Ewelme.
1547	Chantry Certificate.
1551/2	Inventory of church goods.
1554	Richard Beauforest of Dorchester, having bought the Abbey buildings and precinct, bequeathed the eastern part of the abbey church to the parish, his body to be buried in the Lady Aisle.
late 16th century	Feast of St Birinus (3 December) added to Roman martyrology.
1602	West tower rebuilt.
17th century (dates uncertain)	North transept partly demolished. Remaining half and one of its chapels incorporated into north chancel aisle. New window in 'Churchwarden Gothic' inserted.

1633	South nave aisle roof reconstructed.
	William Davey leases property at Overy. The Daveys were Dorchester's leading Catholic family, and Overy became an important centre of recusant worship.
1651/2	Fettiplace grammar school founded in former abbey guest house.
before 1657	Anthony Wood draws plan of church and describes it and precinct.
1673	Anglican authorities record meetings of a 'Phanatick brood' of Protestant nonconformists (probably Congregationalists) in a barn at Overy. Anabaptists, Quakers, Sabbatarians and Independents also recorded in Warborough or Dorchester in the late 1660s and 1670s.
1676	Compton Census records 260 conformists, 6 papists and 13 Nonconformists at Dorchester; 63 conformists and 3 papists at Burcot.
1736	Main road through Dorchester turnpiked.
1739	South chancel aisle roof reconstructed.
1745	Chancel refitted; new reredos, repaving and (?) lowered ceilings cutting across great east window.
1747 and 1760s	Nave roof (east) and nave roof (west) rebuilt.

5. The abbey has attracted the interest of successive generations of antiquarians, who have drawn on the work of their predecessors since the seventeenth century. This sketch plan of 1768, apparently made by Richard Gough and based on that in Stevens' edition of Dugdale's 'Monasticon', appears itself to have been taken from Anthony Wood's plan of 1657. (The Bodleian Library, University of Oxford, Gough Maps 26, fol. 42v)

1792	Church re-pewed.
1796	Dissenting chapel in Dorchester licensed (probably Baptist).
1813–15	Building of new bridge; approach road cut through lower churchyard and toll cottage built.
1819	First Sunday school recorded.

Revival, restoration and change

1835	Anglican National school for girls and infants established.
1837	Baptist chapel built.
1839	Primitive Methodist chapel built.
1844	Oxford Architectural Society begins campaign for restoration of abbey.
1844–6	James Cranston, architect.
	South chancel window and sedilia and north chancel window restored.
1847–58	William Butterfield, architect.
	Work in chancel, including restored east window, new tiling in sanctuary, and new furnishings (chancel stalls, nave pews, pulpit).
1849	New Roman Catholic church of St Birinus opened.
1856	Revd William Macfarlane begins incumbency lasting until 1885, with profound effects on the building and the wider role of the abbey.
1857	New vicarage built.
1858–78	Sir George Gilbert Scott, architect.
	North chancel aisle, south aisle, south chancel aisle, tower and belfry restored. Extensive decoration, including chancel and sanctuary. New heating. New organ.
1858	Abbey guest house becomes National school for boys.
1868	Dorchester becomes titular vicarage instead of perpetual curacy.
1869	School-church opened at Burcot.
1871	New National school for girls and infants.
1878	Missionary Training College opened.
1882	J. H. Parker's *History of Dorchester* published.
1902	Mission room opened by Church Association to counteract high church ritualism of then vicar, Nathaniel Poyntz.
1939	New suffragan bishopric of Dorchester created.
1940	Missionary Training College closed.
1958	North chancel aisle reordered as St Birinus Chapel.
1960	First Dorchester Abbey Festival.

6. The abbey church from the south, c.1910. The bridge, from which the photograph is taken, had been built in 1813–15. Since then, the main road traffic through Dorchester had dwindled and the toll-house become redundant. The abbey, in contrast, had been restored and its influence on all aspects of local life greatly expanded. (© Oxfordshire County Council Photographic Archive)

1961–70	Major appeal for funds, with Edith Stedman in leading role.
	Museum and tea room created in abbey guest house. Cloister memorial garden established.
	Shrine of St Birinus reconstructed (1964) in south chancel aisle; east window restored (1966).
1962	Anglican church of St Mary and St Berin built to serve new settlement of Berinsfield.
1974	Creation of Dorchester team ministry.
1976	Abbey closed for urgent repairs.
1979	Joint pilgrimage to Winchester by Anglican vicar and Roman Catholic priest of Dorchester, marking the 1300th anniversary of West Saxon bishopric moving from Dorchester to Winchester. Annual ecumenical pilgrimages to Dorchester in the steps of St Birinus began in the 1970s and continue.
1980–1	Organ overhauled and moved to new gallery created on the north side of the crossing. New vestry created.

1986–9	Bells restored; chancel repaired and pulpit moved.
1989–93	Abbey guest house restored and new meeting room created.
1989	Exchange link established with Jouarre, home of Agilbert, second bishop of Dorchester (c.650–60).
2000–6	Millennium appeal for major restoration and development of the abbey and its facilities.
March 2005	Institution of Revd Sue Booys, first woman incumbent, as team rector of Dorchester.

These bare bones begin to suggest some of the themes that make Dorchester's history so significant for residents and visitors, archaeologists and historians alike. These include the possibility of links, of site or of faith, between the Roman and the Saxon; the location and plan of the Anglo-Saxon cathedral and whether any of it survives; how and when the medieval church developed, for canons, pilgrims and parishioners; and the relationship between abbey and local people. Changes to the former abbey church and its surroundings in the period after the Dissolution and the Reformation need to be unravelled. How, too, did theological and institutional shifts, the emergence of other churches and chapels, and an element of indifference affect the abbey and Dorchester? More recently the great movements of revival and restoration, modernization and secularization have had an impact clearly to be seen in the buildings and history of the parish and the village.

In the following chapters this summary skeleton will be fleshed out by a team of specialist contributors, whose skills range from archaeology, to architectural studies and social and religious history – a variety of approaches all very relevant to an understanding of this remarkable building.

The archaeological setting of the abbey is discussed by Graham Keevill, who in 2000–1 led the most recent excavations on the abbey site. The historical context of the Saxon cathedrals and medieval abbey is unfolded by James Bond and Kate Tiller and related to successive stages of building and rebuilding of the church. Nicholas Doggett shows how the entire abbey church unusually survived the Dissolution and the Reformation to become the local parish church and looks at its mixed fortunes up to the end of the eighteenth century. Geoffrey Tyack considers the transformation of the abbey church and its worship by nineteenth-century restorations, which have done much to mould the present-day appearance of the abbey. The final two, historical chapters use the increasing wealth of direct records to look at the life of the abbey and its surrounding community. Kate Tiller uncovers the transition from relative decay to religious revival and energetic pastoral action experienced in the nineteenth-century parish. She also reflects on the changing and varied faces of religion – Roman Catholic, nonconformist and Anglican – in post-Reformation Dorchester. And Nicholas Dudley brings the story up to the present day in his account of the abbey between 1920 and 2005.

The aim of this study is to provide an up-to-date overview, which will be illuminating and useful in itself and also act as a starting point for those wanting to find out more from the increasing mass of detailed research. The book ends with a chapter bringing together findings on the surviving fabric of the abbey and inviting the reader to visit the building afresh.

Chapter Two

The Archaeology of Dorchester Abbey

GRAHAM KEEVILL

Important historic monuments deserve – and usually receive – respect and protection, both officially through legal designations or planning controls, and by the care and attention of the people who use them. Nevertheless, very few such places can be 'preserved in aspic', even if there were a wish for this to be done. Buildings have needs – repair and maintenance – and so do the people who use them. Today's churches and their congregations, under pressure from so many directions, try hard to be warm, welcoming and inclusive – metaphorically and literally. So it was that, in 1999, heating and access improvements were proposed at Dorchester Abbey (or the church of St Peter and St Paul), well known as one of the largest, and therefore coldest, parish churches in the Diocese of Oxford.

Naturally enough for such a historically significant building, the proposal required a careful and measured archaeological response. The results more than repaid the effort, providing the first solid evidence for St Birinus's cathedral foundation and much new information about the late Saxon cathedral and the medieval abbey.

A full report has been published elsewhere,[1] and the following outline is written as a contribution to this general history of the abbey. The chapter begins with a brief survey of the archaeology of Dorchester, followed by a description of past archaeological research at the abbey. This leads in to the results of the work carried out in 2001.

Archaeology in and around Dorchester to AD 635

The flat, well-drained gravel terraces of the upper Thames valley to the east of the Sinodun Hills have been attractive for human settlement for many thousands of years, and there is abundant archaeological evidence for this (see Fig. 1). A few finds of palaeolithic material have been made to the north of the village, largely as a result of gravel quarrying, and it is partly because of this destructive process that we know of the neolithic ritual/religious monuments known as cursuses and henges in the same area. The remaining parts of the cursus between quarries can still be seen in aerial photographs. Several items of Bronze Age weaponry have been recovered from the Thames at or near Dorchester, while two of the area's best-known earthwork sites belong to the subsequent Iron Age. First, there is the hill fort on Castle Hill, dominating the lowlands from the Sinodun Hills. This site had not been excavated until recently, when Oxford Archaeology began an important campaign of archaeological research on it in 2003. Secondly, and perhaps most importantly, there is the late Iron Age *oppidum* at Dyke Hills, a substantial town-like settlement on the bank of the Thames. The massive earth ramparts of the settlement are its most obvious feature, but antiquarian and archaeological research have also provided information about circular huts in its interior and numerous finds of gold or silver coins.[2]

Dorchester lies west of the River Thame, near to its confluence with the Thames. General

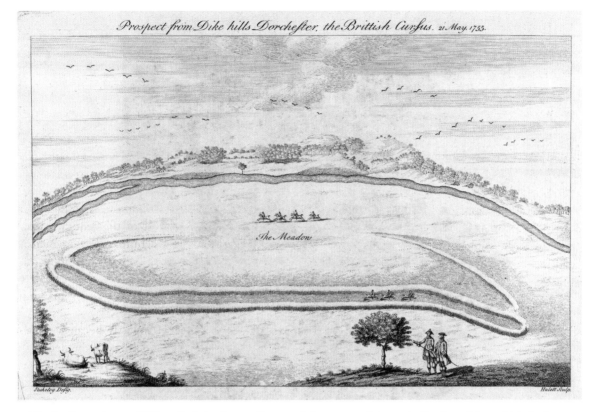

Prospect from Dike hills Dorchester, the Brittish Cursus. 21 May 1755.

The Meadow

Stukeley Delin. *Hulett Sculp.*

7. The leading antiquary, William Stukeley is one of many scholars to speculate on the function of the prehistoric sites around Dorchester. Here, in 1755, he portrays the 'Brittish' cursus in use for horse races, with two debating scholars in the foreground. (The Bodleian Library, University of Oxford, Gough Maps 26, fol. 42v)

topography was important, with the late Iron Age oppidum at Dyke Hills tucked into the bend of the Thames just west of the confluence. As the Roman conquest and occupation of the south-east lowlands of England unfolded, new roads were established to ease military (and subsequently civilian) transport and communication. Two roads, coming north from Winchester and Silchester respectively, converged on the Thames/Thame confluence before continuing north to Alchester, which is now known to be the site of a very early Roman fort, and subsequently a town, the most important Roman settlement in the northern half of the (modern) county.[3] The strategic importance of the road junction at the rivers'

confluence, next to a regionally important and substantial Iron Age settlement, would have made it a prime site for another fort, and one does indeed seem to have been established here, probably after AD 60. Surprisingly little is known of the fort, though it may have lain to the south of the later Roman town. The town may have grown in response to the fort's existence, as was commonly the case, although again little is currently known of its foundation date and impetus to develop. It was certainly in existence in the form we understand today – that is to say, surrounded by an earthwork bank and ditch – by the later second century AD.

Possible continuities at Dorchester between the late Roman and the Anglo-Saxon periods have long fascinated historians. Unfortunately we do not know whether there was a Christian church in the late Roman town, but as Trevor Rowley noted in 1985, it is 'tempting . . . to speculate on a similar [late Roman] origin for the [abbey] church at Dorchester'.[4] This possibility may be corroborated by the presence of fourth- and fifth-century burials on east-west alignments and with no grave goods in the Queenford Mill and Church Piece extra-mural cemeteries.[5] These have generally been interpreted as Christian, although this cannot be regarded as proven. Other late Roman and early post-Roman burials from cemeteries around Dorchester (or more specifically Anglo-Saxon artefacts from them) have been taken as evidence for contact between native Romano-British people and the incoming 'invaders' from continental Europe.[6] Certainly the archaeological evidence does seem to demonstrate continuing activity in and around Dorchester well after the formal withdrawal of the Roman legions (and therefore governance) in AD 410.

The archaeology of the abbey and its surroundings

The medieval abbey church lies close to the Roman town, even – some have argued – within its area. There remains uncertainty over the full extent of the Roman town.[7] The earthwork defences survive along its west side, while the north and south sides are also well known. The location of the eastern rampart, however, has never been established. Two alternative views exist. The first suggests that it ran north–south, a little to the west of the abbey site. This, however, omits a significant promontory of higher ground jutting out into the Thames and Thame floodplain, leading to the alternative suggestion that this area, too, was enclosed by the defences. The former interpretation gives a relatively small,

elongated rectangular 'playing card' shape, while the latter provides a less regular but larger area. The nineteenth-century discovery of a Roman cremation burial in the vicarage garden just to the north of the Cloister Garden provided limited support for the first idea. Under Roman law people could not be buried within settlements, and the cremation site would therefore have lain beyond the urban limits.

The only previous archaeological investigation of the abbey took place in the Cloister Garden in 1960–2, when three small trenches were excavated. These showed that medieval levels survived across much of the area, although they had been affected to varying degrees by post-Dissolution activity.[8] The recovery of large amounts of Roman pottery – apparently in soil layers and features of the same date – also suggested that the site could have lain within the Roman town area. There had been other reports of Roman material from the abbey and its grounds in the nineteenth century, but these were difficult to interpret archaeologically with any certainty. Unfortunately the 1960s trenches provided little or no evidence for the Anglo-Saxon cathedral, though traces of the medieval cloister were found. These had suffered extensive damage after the Dissolution, a common enough fate for monastic buildings that were seen as being little more than quarries for building materials.

The Dorchester Abbey Appeal: archaeological implications

Keeping large churches at a comfortable temperature – or even taking the chill off – used to be a prohibitively expensive business, involving massive boilers and ugly radiators. Modern heating systems, however, are more efficient, cheaper to run and less unsightly. At Dorchester Abbey this meant that a new scheme (first mooted in 1998) of underfloor heating and wall-mounted radiators

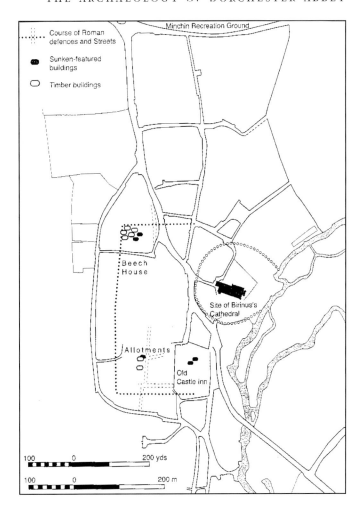

8. Saxon Dorchester, also showing the known course of the Roman defences (Oxoniensia, vol. 68 (2003), p. 256, © OAHS)

could be installed to provide a constant, comfortable background temperature all year round. This would also have significant conservation benefits, by reducing temperature changes and condensation. There was also an opportunity to improve some unsatisfactory aspects of the church's internal arrangements and decoration (see Chapter 7).

The scheme was considered by the Oxford Diocesan Advisory Committee (the Church's own planning authority), English Heritage, the local planning authorities and others. It was decided that the new boiler had to be housed outside the church, in the Cloister Garden on the

north side of the nave, where the monastic cloister had stood. This was an archaeologically sensitive area. The boiler room had to be sunk into the ground by almost 2 m from the existing surface level – a depth that would inevitably disturb archaeological deposits. Furthermore, the room would occupy one end of a newly constructed 'pentice' – a timber-framed building running the full length of the north wall of the nave, and very similar in style to how the medieval cloister might have looked. It would also contain a disabled toilet, a great improvement on existing facilities. The pentice needed new foundations, gas, water and drains, while there was also the underfloor heating inside the church to deal with, all requiring scrutiny by the archaeologists.

Archaeological investigations were carried out before and during the building works. Ground radar surveys in 1999–2000 inside the nave and in the Cloister Garden suggested where the most sensitive areas might be, and trial trenches were dug early in 2001 to confirm this. The trenches seemed to show that the top 0.8–1 m of soil in the Cloister Garden was of little archaeological interest, but it was a different matter below this. Medieval graves were found in each of the three external trenches, while Roman pottery was much in evidence. It was therefore agreed that the boiler room should be excavated archaeologically during early summer 2001 before building work began, while the same archaeologists would be present to check the builders' excavations during the second half of the same year. Thus important new insights into the site's long history were gained without impeding the work.

Archaeological discoveries inside and outside the church

Prehistoric and Roman evidence

Finding a few neolithic or Bronze Age pieces of flint was no great surprise – such material is widely present in Oxfordshire – but there was nothing else to suggest that the site had been used during these periods. By contrast the single Iron Age find was a pleasant surprise. A gold coin dated to around AD 20 was found in an Anglo-Saxon ditch. The coin is of a well-known type often described as 'Cunobelin's Gold', after the tribal chieftain of the Catuvellauni. One side is decorated with an ear of corn flanked by the letters CAM for Camulodunum (Cunobelin's base at Colchester, Essex). The other has the stylized figure of a horse, quite similar to the White Horse at Uffington, with letters CUN (for Cunobelin)

9. The Iron Age gold coin of around AD 20 found during the 2001 excavations on the abbey site (enlarged)

beneath it. This design is common in various forms on these coins, and is a very debased version of a Greek original showing a chariot being pulled by two (or sometimes four) horses. The Dorchester variant is very rare – only four other examples are known. What looks like a wheel can be seen in front of the horse, possibly a last trace of the otherwise forgotten chariot. Perhaps here we have an Iron Age cart before the horse! Many other examples of Cunobelin's gold (and silver) are known from Dorchester (especially Dyke Hills), along with coins from the Dobunni and Silures, tribes based in Gloucestershire and Berkshire respectively.

Interesting new light was thrown by the excavations on the vexed question of where Roman Dorchester's eastern defences lay. As already mentioned, the 1960s trenches and our own trial work earlier in 2001 yielded plenty of Roman finds, including pottery, tiles and a few coins. Indeed several thousand Roman potsherds were found in 2001, with a cumulative weight of about 30 kg; in contrast only 339 pieces (5.5 kg) of Anglo-Saxon, medieval or later pottery were found. By the time we had finished the excavations, however, it was clear that not a single feature of Roman date had been found – no pits, ditches, buildings or anything else. All of the Roman material came from soil layers of later date. The area of investigation was relatively small, of course, but it does now seem more likely that the Roman defences lay to the west of the Cloister Garden. The area between the town and the River Thame would thus have been open ground, and may have been used as a dumping ground for domestic rubbish.

A recent (2005) survey of the fabric of the abbey by Dr Warwick Rodwell[9] and associated evidence reinforce the conclusion that the boundary of the Roman town ran north–south to the west of the current abbey site. Rodwell considers it strange that, given that many early Christian churches were founded inside the walled enclosures of Roman towns, Birinus shunned such an area in almost certainly establishing his cathedral at Dorchester outside the ramparts. Rodwell further notes that the ground where the abbey now stands, on a brick earth and gravel knoll, with the river flowing to the east and the ground gently sloping away in all directions, would be a curious exclusion from the area of the Roman town unless something else was already there. He hypothesizes that this could have been a Roman temple and its precinct, basing his case on analogy with other Roman towns, particularly Chelmsford (Essex), and finds on or near the abbey site, including an early-third-century altar, tesserae from pavements, and the burial in the vicarage garden. The presence of a Roman temple, precinct and burial place on the site of the abbey remains an intriguing speculation, which only further evidence from study of artefacts and excavation will confirm or refute.

The Anglo-Saxon period – looking for Dorchester Cathedral
The lower levels of excavation in the boiler room and elsewhere proved to be of the Anglo-Saxon era, representing use of the site from the sixth to the eleventh centuries. This historic period is notoriously difficult to date archaeologically, especially in its earliest stages (that is to say, the fifth and sixth centuries AD). We normally rely on artefacts such as coins and pottery for dating evidence, but they are very scarce over these two centuries. Even when pottery did become more commonly used, from the seventh century onwards, the shapes and decorative styles tended to be long-lasting and thus difficult to date accurately. Despite these limitations, a clear sequence of building development was recognized in the boiler-room excavation. Similar sequences of buildings have been found at three other sites in Dorchester. The more limited trenching elsewhere made it impossible to identify any other buildings positively, though their presence is at least implicit from the discovery of soil layers similar to those found within the boiler-room structures. The following description relates entirely to the boiler room.

The earliest Anglo-Saxon building was of a kind well known to archaeologists, a sunken-featured building – or more prosaically a 'grub-hut', or *grubenhaus*, because it was based on a simple pit hollowed out of the ground surface (in this instance the underlying brick earth). An equally simple tent-like superstructure was usually defined by a frame of post-holes supporting a roof, probably of thatch. Only part of the Dorchester example lay within the boiler room, but it was large for its type, at least 4.7 m – from east to west – by 3.7 m. The hollow area was about 0.2 m deep, and several narrow slots dug into its floor suggested that a timber floor had been built over it. An area of charred timber found along the east edge was probably a remnant of the floor.

The building lay at right angles to the abbey nave, and had been cut away by it. It was in use in the period before Birinus's mission in 635. We cannot be sure how long it continued, but at some time during the seventh or eighth century it was replaced by a quite different building. This used a form of timber framing, with the uprights of the wall set into a continuous trench. Clearly it was more sophisticated than the early hut, both architecturally and in building techniques. Only one wall lay within the excavations, but we could be certain that this was the west side – floors and occupation debris were found inside the building on the east side of the wall, while there was nothing to the west. The building was briefly abandoned, perhaps during the ninth century, before being rebuilt in the same position and using the same techniques, but slightly further to the north. Once again, internal floors were found to the east of the exterior wall, while a boundary ditch was found running parallel with, and just to the west of, the structure. The Iron Age gold coin was found in this ditch, along with unusual post-Roman pottery, possibly of eastern Mediterranean origin.

The later of the two successive timber-framed structures apparently continued in use into the eleventh century, perhaps to the final years of the cathedral. We assume that the building and ditch went out of use at the same time, though the archaeology cannot determine this. At any rate the ditch had certainly been backfilled deliberately,

and the digging of a large pit had subsequently removed its north end. The pit could not be fully excavated – coring showed that it continued for at least 0.65 m beneath the base of the boiler room – but its function was clear enough. A stone-lined well shaft was found slightly off-centre on the west side. This was the latest Anglo-Saxon feature excavated, and may have continued in use into the Norman period.

It is clear that the middle and later Anglo-Saxon features discovered by the excavation were in use while Dorchester was a cathedral, i.e. before 1072. Are any walls of the present church of the same period? Despite close attention during 2001, evidence for Anglo-Saxon masonry within the surviving walls and foundations proved elusive. The eastern end of the nave north wall contains a very large, circular-headed blocked arch, robbed of its stone dressings. Work based on an orthophotographic survey of this and the west end of the north aisle has reconstructed this Anglo-Saxon arch, and suggested that it led from the nave or crossing of the Saxon cathedral into a porticus, or side chamber, the west wall of

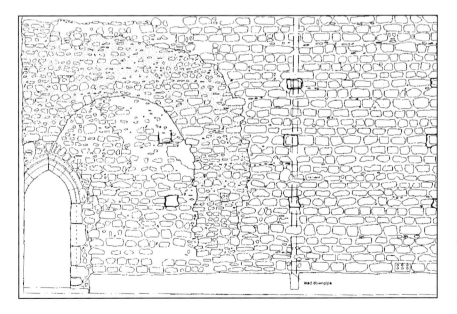

10. Elevation of the eastern half of the north wall of the nave, showing three structural phases. The rubblework defining the semicircular arch on the left (stippled) is Anglo-Saxon; the regularly coursed masonry with rows of putlog holes is early Norman (11th century); and the small pointed doorway on the extreme left is a 14th-century insertion. (Drawing by Caroline Atkins)

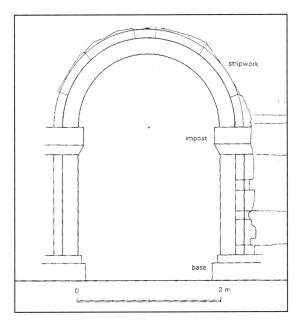

11. Reconstruction of the lost ashlar lining of the Anglo-Saxon arch in the north wall of the nave. The impost and base mouldings are notional, but the divisions in the stripwork are ghosted in surviving fabric.

the present north aisle probably incorporating parts of the east wall of the porticus. This is certainly one of the earliest features so far identified. A trial pit excavated inside the nave also suggested that the same wall's foundations included some early, perhaps pre-Norman, material. The 1999 radar survey hinted at walls of a similar kind underlying the nave floor. This is the limit of our current knowledge of the cathedral that was founded by Birinus and used until the 1070s.

So much for the cathedral itself. What of the buildings excavated in the boiler room? The early hut seems to pre-date the foundation of the cathedral, at least in its origin, though it may have remained in use for some time after that. The two later timber-framed buildings, unlike the early grub-hut, lay at a distinct angle to the nave on an exact north-south alignment. It seems clear that they were not part of the church itself (though there is a slight chance that they were porticus, or

side-rooms, off the main part of the building). The evidence from the internal floors and occupation layers points strongly towards a domestic function. They may have provided accommodation for clergy or secular folk serving within the cathedral and they were certainly within its precinct. Furthermore, this seems to have been separated off into individual areas, if the evidence of the boundary ditch is anything to go by. Much archaeological work has been carried out on Anglo-Saxon cathedrals like Canterbury and Winchester over the last thirty to forty years, but remarkably little is known of their precincts. We do know something of contemporary monastic enclosures, and in that sense the Dorchester evidence is similar to what has been found at Hartlepool (Cleveland), Whitby (North Yorkshire) and Whithorn (Dumfries and Galloway).[10]

The medieval abbey

The decades following the Norman conquest saw Dorchester lose its cathedral status and graduate towards the monastic life of the Augustinian abbey established in the twelfth century.[11] The collegiate church of the secular canons (c.1072–1140) is difficult to recognize archaeologically. We may presume that the greater part of the cathedral buildings continued in use, including the church. Some alterations may have been necessary, but wholesale reconstruction was probably unnecessary, and perhaps beyond the means of the new community. The most recent excavations tell us something of the domestic arrangements within the cathedral precinct, but the Anglo-Saxon church of Birinus and his successors is elusive. So too, therefore, is anything to do with the secular canons, if all they did was occupy the old cathedral. The early masonry at the east end of the nave's north wall, and parts of the latter's foundations, appear to be Saxo-Norman, and could belong to the cathedral and/or the secular

12. Fragments of moulded stone found during the 2001 excavations suggest that the west end of the Norman abbey had doors and windows decorated with zigzag and beaked heads, similar to the west front of Iffley church, Oxford, shown here

many further alterations during the thirteen and fourteenth centuries, and these often had the effect of obscuring or even removing architectural features of the twelfth-century church. While substantial areas of masonry of that date survive, therefore, there are only a couple of windows and doors to go with them. Fortunately the Norman architectural details were completely redundant by the time they were replaced with new doors or windows, so that the removed stonework was only good for re-use in general masonry or for discard. Many fine pieces of moulded stone – especially from arches – were simply thrown away. The abbey already contained a substantial collection of these, gathered over the course of the nineteenth and twentieth centuries. Several more pieces were found during the 2001 excavations and watching brief, and the collection shows that the west end of the Norman abbey would have had elaborately decorated doors and windows featuring zigzag mouldings and beaked heads. The use of this style of decoration flourished from 1125 to 1150. Fragments from Reading Abbey can be seen in Reading museum and, better still, *in situ* on the famous west end of the church of St Mary the Virgin, Iffley (Oxford), giving a good impression of how Dorchester Abbey would have looked in the middle of the twelfth century.

Evidence for the Norman rebuilding is not confined to disparate architectural fragments. Foundations, door positions and floors relating to this work were also found inside the church. Some of this was expected, such as the twelfth-century foundations underlying the later (thirteenth- and fourteenth-century) arcade piers in the chancel. Nevertheless, it was valuable to establish how wide (1.4 m maximum) these foundations were, not least because this tallied exactly with the widths recorded for the nave's north and west walls. Furthermore, these observations also confirmed the long-held assumption that the

canons' church (see also Chapter 3). The nave foundations clearly cut through all the Anglo-Saxon timber buildings found in the boiler room, but there is no inherent contradiction here as these foundations were single-phase, dated to the Augustinian rebuilding after 1140. The well, described above, was probably used (if not necessarily dug) by the secular canons, after the 1070s, but little or nothing else can currently be ascribed to their tenure with any certainty.

We have more evidence for what happened in the 1140s once the Augustinians took over and took on the rebuilding that is such a characteristic Norman response to Anglo-Saxon ecclesiastical architecture. However, the abbey underwent

13. Interior of the nave and chancel during the works of 2002–3

twelfth-century church was cruciform in plan, with an elongated eastern arm. Perhaps the most important discovery, however, was at the south-west corner of the nave. A short stretch of the original south wall survives here, running from the corner to the first arch of the arcade that was punched through the wall in the fourteenth century. The surviving wall seems plain and feature-less, though the masonry is rendered. In fact, excavation for the heating ducts along the north (internal) face of the wall exposed a 1.38 m-wide gap in the wall's foundations 2.7 m to the east of the corner. This must be the position of the orig-inal entrance into the Norman nave, redundant

(and therefore blocked up) once an aisle was added to the south side of the nave in the fourteenth century.

Evidence for the medieval cloister was found during all stages of work in 2001. The trial trenches, for instance, located the foundations for the west side of the east cloister walk, a covered corridor running around three sides at least of a central open courtyard. The equivalent founda-tion on the west side of the cloister had been located during the 1960s trial trenching, when the mortar bedding for a pavement (probably tiled) was found in the corridor itself. A short, intact stretch of the west wall of the walk was found in the boiler room in 2001, along with the robber trench running north from it. This was effectively the 'ghost' of the medieval foundations, left behind when they were removed stone by stone and then backfilled with soil after the Dissolution. The same wall also formed one side of a range of buildings running along the west side of the cloister. The other wall of this range was seen in two trenches immediately to the north of the tower. Unfortunately we do not know the function of the buildings here. The east side of a monastic cloister was given over to the chapter house (where the community held daily meetings to discuss liturgy, discipline and other business) and storage for books, vestments and church plate. The monks' dormitory was normally located on the first floor above these rooms. This arrangement was the same, except for minor

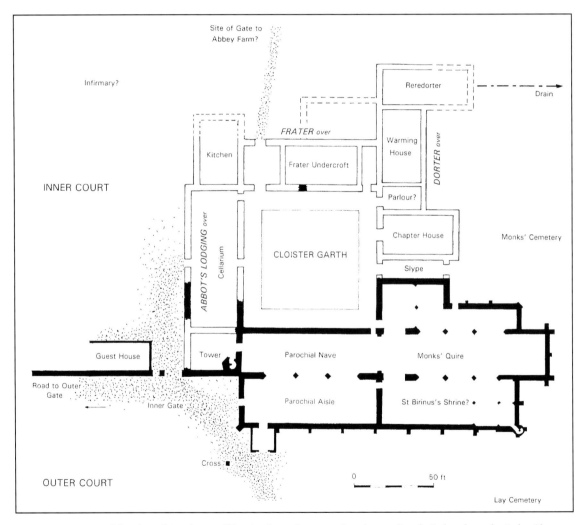

14. Reconstruction of the plan of Dorchester Abbey in the 15th century, based on archaeological and geophysical evidence. The claustral ranges are interpreted by reference to Lacock Abbey, Wiltshire, and other Augustinian houses. Walls shown in solid black are certain.

20

variations, across all the monastic orders. Use of the west range was much less standardized. It might provide housing for guests, storage for food and drink, or private accommodation for the prior. A geophysical survey (2004) of the cloister garden provided further enigmatic traces of former buildings. A hypothetical plan of Dorchester's cloister can be attempted, although more extensive excavation would be necessary to have any chance of identifying the function of Dorchester's west range with certainty.

Cloister walks commonly ran around all four sides of the central courtyard (often used as a garden, especially for herbs), with one side backing directly against the nave, as may have been the case at Dorchester – at least three cut-off timbers can be seen high in the nave north wall just below the cill line of the windows.[12] Two of 2001's three trial trenches in the Cloister Garden suggested a robber trench running east-west parallel to and about 3 m out from the nave wall. The larger excavations, for the boiler room and the rest of the pentice, told a somewhat different story. Burials, predominantly of canons, were found throughout this area, densely packed and extending northwards beyond the limit of excavation. No sign of a foundation or robber trench could be seen. It is possible that there never was a south cloister walk against the nave. We found during the excavation that this space received very little daylight, owing to the height of the nave and tower. The excavations were in shadow by mid-morning, even in the middle of summer. The area against the nave was often used as the *scriptorium*, where manuscript books were written and illuminated. Lack of daylight would hinder this. There is a doorway from the east end of the nave into the cloister, but this would have opened directly into the east cloister walk. It is possible that the medieval burials had been dug into the top of the cloister walk foundations, thus obscuring it (the 'wall' facing into the courtyard would

have been an open arcade, at least during the twelfth and thirteenth centuries).

It is worth dwelling on the position of Dorchester Abbey's cloister for a moment. Medieval cloisters were normally placed to the south of the monastic church to make maximum use of available light and climatic benefits. The north side could be used instead if the site's topography dictated it. What determined such a switch at Dorchester? There is no reason to suppose that it was anything inherent in the underlying geology. Was it merely the sloping site or were two intriguing alternative factors influential? Firstly, the south side of the medieval church is now occupied by a graveyard, closed in the nineteenth century but probably in use throughout the medieval period as the parochial cemetery. It is tempting to think that the graveyard was in use during the Anglo-Saxon period as well, in which case it would have been difficult to build a church over it (but not impossible – something similar occurred at Carlisle Cathedral at about the same time). Secondly, parts of the Anglo-Saxon cathedral (perhaps the church itself) may have lain in the area now occupied by the graveyard. This could well have prevented the construction of a cloister there in the 1140s.

The graves within the Cloister Garden were predominantly medieval. Some 27 skeletons were excavated, with others being exposed but left *in situ* because they were just below the level needed for construction or other work. Most of the 27 were adults, with only three infants or children present. There were very few women. One unfortunate was buried with her unborn child, perhaps having died in the act of birth. Most of the burials were very plain, with only one or two showing any evidence of a coffin. One adult male, buried close against the nave wall, was obviously important, as he had been laid to rest in a solid stone sarcophagus. He may not have been the originally intended occupant,

15. The sarcophagus and the skeleton, with broken legs, crammed into it found by the north nave wall in 2001

or perhaps he gained weight before death, because the hollowed-out part where the body lay had had to be widened to accommodate it. The form of burial suggests that this was one of the medieval abbots, or an important and wealthy patron. Unfortunately there were no grave goods to suggest which was the more likely. More fortunately, this was one case where the coffin and skeleton lay just below the foundation depth. Thus this medieval man at least could be left to rest in peace. The excavated skeletons, meanwhile, must be returned to the ground from whence they came. Re-burial in the same spot is clearly impossible – the pentice has now been built – but they will be kept as close as possible to their first resting place.

Excavation elsewhere was more restricted, but did provide insights into how the monastic precinct was arranged, including its entrance. The lych-gate is a modern feature, but it is easy to assume it might have been built on the site of the main historic entrance, lining up with the late medieval entrances in the south-west corner of the church. A trench excavated from the High Street, through the gate, in front of the late medieval guest house, and around the west side of the tower, gave us the chance to address this question. No road surface was found, but a flint cobbled surface did stretch from just within the lych-gate for 6.5 m eastwards. Rodwell has argued that this was the main entrance way between an outer and inner gatehouse. He bases this on the alignment with the west door of the abbey, the presence in the adjoining lower wall of the guest house of substantial walling potentially belonging to a precinct wall, and the need to separate the entrance for the laity (via an outer precinct) from the area of the cloister (in an inner precinct). An alternative view is that the gatehouse was further to the north on High Street, probably in roughly the position of the current post office. This makes sense on looking carefully at the guest house itself, which is jettied out at first-floor level, but on the north, not the south, side. The purpose of a jetty was to provide greater floor space above the ground floor, where this had to be kept back from a street. Thus the guest house's jetty may imply the presence of an access road on the north side of the building.

It is likely that there was a further gateway between the west tower of the abbey and the guest house. Certainly the latter is now truncated at its east end, with one jamb of a former door at ground floor level and part of a window on the first floor. These show that the building extended eastwards for at least one further bay in the medieval period, and it is quite plausible that it originally joined up with the west end of the abbey. If it did so, there would have been a need for a pedestrian door at least, and probably a second, larger archway, to allow access between the cloister/north precinct and the graveyard on the south side of the church. The rebuilding of the west tower in about 1600 would have presented the opportunity to remove the door/gate and reduce the length of the guest house at the same time, thus facilitating movement around the west end of the church. Unfortunately no traces of buildings or any other archaeological features were present in the service trenches excavated here.

Henry VIII and after: the Dissolution of the Monasteries

The closure of the abbey at the Dissolution, and its rapid resurrection as Dorchester's parish church, is strongly reflected in the archaeology of the site, both internally and externally. The most obvious points are the survival of the church itself, and by contrast the destruction of all other monastic buildings except the guest house. The demolition of the cloister and its surrounding ranges is reflected in the robbed-out foundation trenches, found both in the 1960s and 2001 excavations. The upper soil layers in the Cloister Garden also contained building rubble such as roof tile and stone, though few floor tiles were recovered. Presumably they were removed carefully for reuse elsewhere, perhaps in the church itself. Certainly more pieces of decorated tile were found there, buried under the existing floor in the nave and elsewhere. The current floors contain many post-medieval gravestones, some with interesting (and often moving) inscriptions commemorating the deceased. Not all of them came from the inside of the church originally, and they were all reset in their current locations, probably in the nineteenth century.

This summary of the 2001 excavations ends with one of its least interesting features from a purely archaeological perspective. Insertion of the new heating ducts in the north-west corner of the nave revealed the large, brick-lined underground chamber for the late nineteenth-/early twentieth-century boiler – the last vestige of previous generations' attempts to keep the church warm. (For a description of these heroic efforts, see Chapter 7.) The chamber had been backfilled with rubble when the redundant boiler was removed after the Second World War. The rubble contained several pieces of medieval stonework, including one intact arch stone decorated with a beaked head. This seemed to provide an appropriate bridge between past and present heating arrangements, and the study of the ancient past of this most venerable, beautiful and treasured church.

Chapter Three

Cathedral and Abbey, 635–1536

JAMES BOND AND KATE TILLER

The archaeological record has shown the early significance of the Dorchester area as a focus of settlement, burial and ritual sites from the neolithic to the Iron Age, to the Roman and pagan Anglo-Saxon. The first entry of Dorchester in the written record describes its major new status, as the first Christian bishopric and cathedral in the freshly converted kingdom of the West Saxons. As Bede, in his *Ecclesiastical History of the English People* (completed in 731),[1] records:

> during the reign of Cynigils, the West Saxons, anciently known as the Gewissae, accepted the Faith of Christ through the preaching of Bishop Birinus. He had come to Britain at the direction of Pope Honorius [I], having promised in his presence that he would sow the seeds of our holy Faith in the most inland and remote regions of the English, where no other teacher had been before him. He was accordingly consecrated bishop by Asterius, Bishop of Genoa, at the Pope's command; but when he had reached Britain and entered the territory of the Gewissae, he found them completely heathen, and decided that it would be better to begin to preach the word of God among them rather than seek more distant converts. He therefore evangelised the province, and when he had instructed its king, he baptised him and his people. It happened at the time that the most holy and victorious Oswald was present, and greeted King Cynigils as he came from the font, and offered him an alliance most acceptable to God, taking him as his godson and

giving his daughter as wife. The two kings gave Bishop Birinus the city of Dorcic [Dorchester] for his episcopal see, and there he built and dedicated several churches and brought many people to God by his holy labours. He also died and was buried there.

The meeting of Cynegils and Oswald at Dorchester brought together two strands of Christian conversion, that from Rome, represented by the Papal missionary Birinus, and that from the Celtic

16. One of the fine watercolours of the abbey done by John Carter in 1792–3 in preparation for his proposed 'Antiquities of Dorchester', which was never published. It shows the stained glass panel of St 'Bernius' preaching, then in the south chancel window (cf. frontispiece). (The Bodleian Library, University of Oxford, Gough Maps 227, fol. 47)

DIOCESAN CHANGES 650 - 1250

| = Dorchester | C = Canterbury | Cr = Crediton | + Location of sees - certain |
| | R = Rochester | E = Exeter | ?⊕ Location of sees - uncertain |

17. During the Saxon period, Dorchester was three times the centre of a diocese

church, represented by Oswald, king of North-umbria (a convert at Iona). The great event was also politically significant. A unified England was still three centuries ahead. Rivalry between king-doms, armed conflict and shifting territorial boundaries were to affect Dorchester throughout that time. In the 630s the kings of the West Saxons and Northumbria had a shared interest in allying against a common enemy, Penda, the aggressive pagan king of the Midland Kingdom of Mercia. Dorchester lay on the then northern boundary of Cynegils' kingdom, well placed on river and road routes. It also conformed to Pope Gregory's injunction to early missionaries to establish dio-ceses in former Roman towns, their bishops gov-erning surrounding territories echoing those of classical times. Certainly Bede accorded Dorches-ter the status of 'civitas', or city, despite its relative-ly modest size and probable influence. As John Blair has put it, Dorchester was 'a place of visible ancient importance at a time when such things were starting to matter again; a dominant military group with aspiration to royal dignity would naturally take control of it.'[2]

From 635 until Birinus's death in 650, Dor-chester remained the only cathedral in West Saxon territory, the centre of a diocese which straddled the middle Thames and extended towards the south coast; but its pre-eminence was short lived. In 643 Cynegils had been succeeded by his son, Cenwalh, a pagan who unwisely abandoned his wife, the sister of Penda of Mercia. Cenwalh was driven into exile when Penda invaded Wessex in 645 and, although he subsequently converted to Christianity and returned to his kingdom, the Mercians had by then gained control of the upper- and mid-Thames valley. Historians have speculated as to what might have happened had Dorchester continued uninterrupted as the cathe-dral town of Wessex: 'but for Penda, the little country town of Dorchester-on-Thames might have become the capital of a united England.'[3] In

fact the power base of Wessex shifted south and a new see was established, at Winchester, in the 660s. The Gaulish bishop, Agilbert, who had been appointed as successor to Birinus, had returned to Gaul and the West Saxon bishopric of Dorchester lapsed in favour of Winchester.

Nothing survives above ground of Birinus's church, and (in the absence of excavated evi-dence) there is debate as to its site.[4] The consen-sus is that it was on, or near, the site of the present abbey. The most likely known parallel is the Old Minster at Winchester, built in c. 648, the restored ground-plan of which can now be seen just north of the present cathedral, begun in 1079. There were probably other religious buildings at Dor-chester. A group of small rectangular timber halls (later rebuilt in stone), excavated in the north-west corner of the Roman town, may represent a pre-Viking monastic site.[5] Bede refers to Birinus building and dedicating 'several churches'. If they were in Dorchester, rather than elsewhere in the see, they suggest a pattern familiar in major ec-clesiastical foundations of the seventh and eighth centuries, that is, an integrated group of two or more churches, axially aligned and perhaps related to other liturgical focuses, such as crosses and wells. Dorchester may have followed this trend.[6] William of Malmesbury in c. 1125 wrote of 'the beauty and state of [Dorchester's] churches',[7] whilst John Leland in 1542[8] mentioned (in the past tense) three parish churches. Rodwell has 'approximately deduced' the location of two of these: one just south of the abbey churchyard on the site of the old Castle Inn, and one at Bridge End at the corner of the green.[9]

Once its position as the West Saxon cathedral ended, Dorchester continued as some kind of religious centre throughout the Saxon period. However, around 690, the remains of Birinus were removed to Winchester, where successive shrines were built to him. Dorchester was to attain cathe-dral status twice more. Briefly, with the adoption of Christianity by the Mercian royal house, a bishop at Dorchester presided over a small south Mercian see, perhaps as early as the mid-660s, certainly in the late 670s; but the bishopric had probably lapsed by 685, when the Thames valley again became a cockpit of conflict between Wessex and Mercia. Mercian ecclesiastical adminis-

tration shifted north, with bishoprics at Leicester and Lindsey (now in Lincolnshire). For two centuries the history of Dorchester is silent and the church seems to have been reduced to the status of a minster. Then, in the 870s, Danish raids smashed the political and military power of Mercia. The Mercian sees of Lindsey and Leicester were

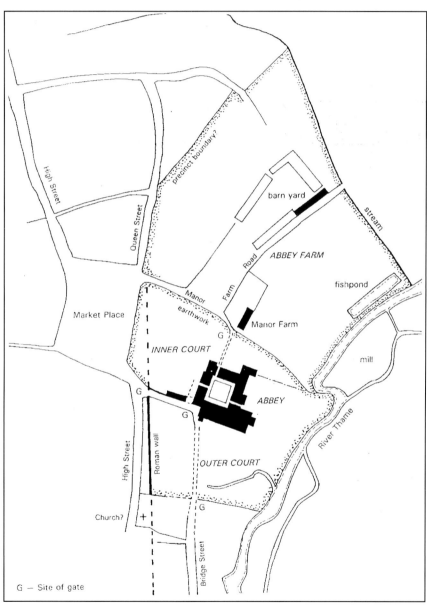

18. Reconstruction of
Dorchester Abbey precincts
in the early 16th century

27

abandoned and never re-established. Once more Dorchester became the seat of a Mercian bishop, his diocese, the largest in England, stretching from the Thames to the Humber and persisting until the Norman conquest (see Fig. 17).

The continuing ecclesiastical importance of Dorchester throughout the tenth and eleventh centuries must have demanded a significant building, most likely of stone. As we have seen,[10] archaeologists, antiquaries and architectural historians have hunted for signs of Dorchester's Saxon cathedral since the seventeenth century. The view that the late Saxon cathedral was on the present site and that some small part of it does survive within the present fabric has been reinforced by recent excavation and survey work. A picture emerges of a narrow, proportionately tall, unaisled building of cruciform plan. The position of one lateral arm of the plan is established by the ghost archway in the present abbey's north nave wall. This led to a porticus, or side chamber, now lost but with an estimated minimum width of 5 m.[11]

The Saxon cathedral was part of a wider local landscape. The presence of groups of Saxon buildings, excavated within the walls of the Roman town, has already been mentioned, as have Dorchester's (three?) parish churches. The cathedral lay in a precinct to the east of the Roman ramparts. That ecclesiastical precinct expanded to the west, its presence influencing the plan of the adjoining town, effectively pulling the line of the main street to the east, away from the north–south axial route between gates of the Roman town. The line of the present High Street thus shifted to pass the entrance to the ecclesiastical precinct, near which a market place probably developed. Its area was encroached on by building from the late middle ages. This replanning drew settlement away from the southern sector of the old town and although it cannot be precisely dated, it is likely to have happened in the late Saxon or Norman periods. A final feature to note

is that the abbey building is skewed by twenty degrees from the east–west axis, raising the interesting possibility that it was aligned with other pre-existing features to the west of the site.[12] This hypothesis awaits further landscape analysis. The fact that the post-Conquest church at Dorchester was not (like Winchester and other major churches) realigned 'correctly' by the Normans is further evidence that it adopted the site of the Saxon cathedral.

In 1067 the last Saxon bishop of Dorchester, Wulfwig, died. He was succeeded by the Norman Remigius, who styled himself Bishop of Dorchester, Leicester and Lincoln. Within five years, following a general decree to move the seats of bishops to large towns, Dorchester was one of the places to lose its cathedral status, in its case to Lincoln. Dorchester's inherited importance, lent it by antiquity and the political circumstances of the seventh century, had been overtaken by a new, urban geography of centres of ecclesiastical and secular power. Locally Wallingford and Oxford had both become more important than Dorchester, whilst nearby Benson was the biggest royal vill in Saxon Oxfordshire.

The period 1067 to 1072 is a very short time in Dorchester's history, yet William of Malmesbury and later scholars think it likely that, in true Norman fashion, Remigius began to rebuild Dorchester cathedral. Rodwell, in his survey of 2005, concludes that 'much of the ground plan, the lower half of the nave walls, and parts of the south transept date from the Saxo-Norman era, and are potentially assignable to Bishop Remigius's rebuild.'[13] This was the church that continued to be used by the secular canons after the removal of the see to Lincoln.

The monastic era

For some seventy years after the removal of the see to Lincoln, Dorchester remained a collegiate church of secular canons, typical of many un-reformed ecclesiastical communities of the late Saxon period. They undertook pastoral duties, whilst living in separate households with a relatively undemanding daily routine.

Around 1140 Alexander, Bishop of Lincoln (1123–48), replaced the secular canons at Dorchester with a group of thirteen regular canons following the Augustinian rule, and a stricter way of life was introduced. It was the last of a series of religious foundations made by the bishop and coincided with a peak of Augustinian growth in England. The canons at Dorchester were members of an autonomous group within the Augustinian family, the Arrouaisians. This group developed from a hermit colony established at Arrouaise near Bapaume in the diocese of Amiens, which had been reorganized under Abbot Gervase (1121–47) into an influential house of regular canons with strict observances, partly borrowed from Cistercian customs. Arrouaisians wore a white habit, abstained from meat eating, practised manual labour and kept silence. The order began to spread beyond France in the 1130s and twenty-four English houses eventually had some connection with it.[14]

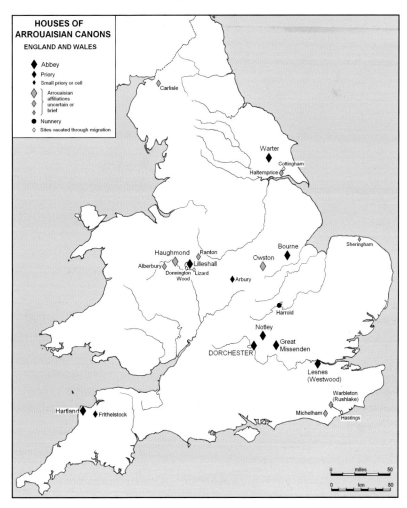

19. Dorchester Abbey was founded in c.1140 as a house of Arrouaisian canons, an autonomous group within the Augustinian family

Sadly no cartulary, chronicle or account rolls survive from Dorchester Abbey. The house had the status of a self-governing abbey. Its possessions were confirmed by Papal bull in 1146 and 1163.[15] The Augustinian canons had particularly strong links with parish churches and Dorchester's endowment was heavily balanced towards parochial income from tithes, glebe land and mortuary fees (known as 'spiritualities'). When, in 1291, Pope Nicholas IV taxed ecclesiastical incomes to support Edward I's projected crusade to the Holy Land, Dorchester's income proved to be unusually dependent on monies from 'spiritualities' (£58 18s 4d) as opposed to

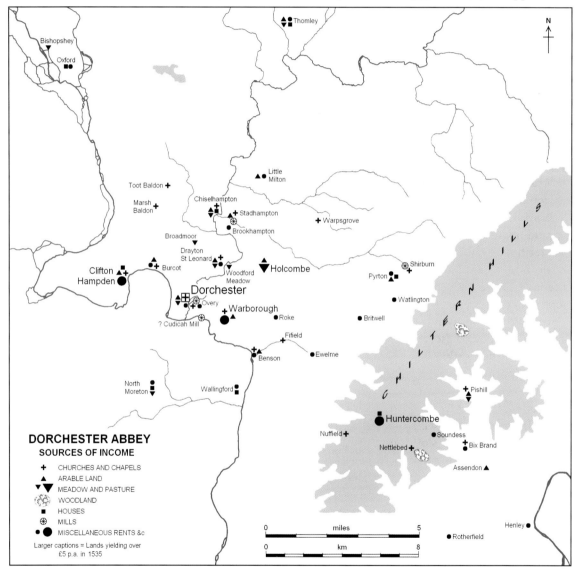

DORCHESTER ABBEY
SOURCES OF INCOME

+ CHURCHES AND CHAPELS
▲ ARABLE LAND
▼▼ MEADOW AND PASTURE
WOODLAND
■ HOUSES
✪ MILLS
•● MISCELLANEOUS RENTS &c

Larger captions = Lands yielding over
£5 p.a. in 1535

20. The abbey had active connections with many local places, serving their churches or owning property. From the Dissolution to the 1830s, Dorchester was to remain the centre of an ecclesiastical jurisdiction (the Peculiar) reflecting these earlier links.

'temporalities', income from demesne lands and rents (£26 1s 4d).[16] Both meant that Dorchester Abbey had close and long-running links with a large number of local communities. Local churches and chapels were given to it, including Chiselhampton, Clifton Hampden, Drayton St Leonard, Stadhampton and Toot Baldon, all of which had been part of the ancient endowment of the cathedral. The canons were also directly responsible for serving the parochial needs of Dorchester itself. The splendid font, one of the outstanding features of the abbey, is also evidence of these pastoral responsibilities. It is datable on art-historical grounds to c.1170–80, one of only twenty-nine lead fonts surviving in England and the only one from a monastic church.[17] The figures of eleven haloed Apostles are seated below an arcade, with continuous borders of foliage at the top and bottom of the bowl.

A priority for the canons was to create a cloister and its associated buildings, including the chapter house, refectory and dormitory, essential to life under monastic rule. We have seen how recent archaeological investigations and comparisons with other better-documented Augustinian sites enable a reconstruction of the likely claustral layout at Dorchester (see Fig. 14). The cloister's location on the north, rather than the south, of the abbey church continues to attract speculation (see also p. 21). Did this simply follow the lie of the ground, as at the Arrouaisian house of Lesnes (now Greater London), whose north-side cloister is attributed to a steep slope and the necessities of drainage, or did pre-existing features at Dorchester preclude building to the south?

By the late twelfth century attention had turned to the church, and increasingly to the east end, where divine office was performed. This was to become the crowning architectural glory of the abbey. The inherited collegiate church was long, narrow, cruciform and unaisled, with two almost matching transepts. The chancel was slightly narrower than the nave: its length is unknown, but there is no evidence of an apse or of a stone crossing tower (Fig. 24.1).

Architectural evidence of the early stages of the Augustinian rebuilding (Fig. 24.2) survives in the chancel arch, in Transitional style of c.1175, with an unmoulded pointed arch with slender shafts and capitals with palmette leaves. The nave remained little changed, with tall, round-headed

21. The font of c.1170–80. This notable Norman lead font, decorated with seated figures holding books and assumed to be Apostles, was painted by Carter in 1792–3. It then rested on a medieval base, probably contemporary with the 14th-century south aisle and replaced in the 1870s. (The Bodleian Library, University of Oxford, Gough Maps 227, fol. 35)

22. The south crossing arch cuts through the earlier, Romanesque string-course. The original north, south and east arches of the crossing were displaced by the 14th-century additions to the east end, seen in the background.

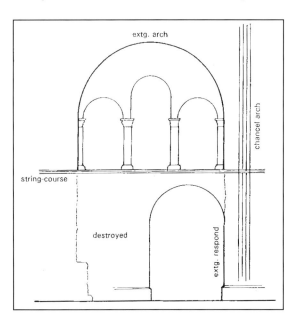

23. Suggested reconstruction of the Norman south crossing arch and arcaded gallery opening above

windows, regularly spaced a rod (16½ feet, or 5 m) apart. The Romanesque string-course in the north and south walls runs through the nave and crossing, showing how they were united when the chancel arch was built. The arch was then the western arch of the crossing, the eastern arch of which must have lain where the string-course ends. The transept arches to the north and south, now tall, plain and round-headed, have long puzzled architectural historians, who have dated them to various periods between the pre-Conquest and the eighteenth century. Nicholas Doggett reviews evidence from the seventeenth and eighteenth centuries in Chapter 4 (see pp. 45-6). Elsewhere both Thurlby[18] and Rodwell[19] have recently concluded that there were no tall, open arches to the north and south in the late twelfth century. Rather the north and south sides of the crossing were probably divided into two stories, a wider upper arch containing recessed sub-arches at the higher level and, below, an off-centre opening into each transept. It is possible that each transept was also two-storied. Beyond the eastern crossing arch a new monastic choir was built. It was only after the south chancel aisle was developed in later, fourteenth-century rebuilding that the eastern arch and the eastern walls of the former transepts were removed (Fig. 24.7). They consider that the present tall lateral arches were created to fill the resulting gaps, probably in the late middle ages.

The first rebuilding of the church as an abbey was soon followed by more, increasingly ambitious work. A seminal event at this time (one of the few in the medieval history of the church for which a dated record exists) was the grant of papal approval for the translation of the relics of St Birinus 'to a more worthy place'.[20] The request to Pope Honorius III had been a problem. The remains of Birinus were stated by Bede to have been taken to Winchester in the late seventh century and had been venerated there in successive

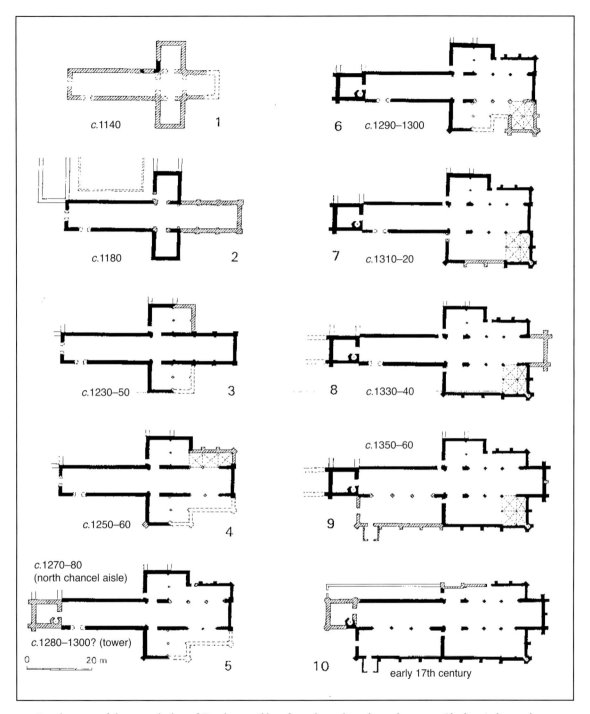

24. *Development of the ground-plan of Dorchester Abbey, from the 11th to the 17th century. Shading indicates the new work at each phase, while black denotes masonry retained from a previous phase. (After Rodwell)*

shrines. Archbishop Langton of Canterbury was asked by the Pope to investigate and heard how, some fifty years earlier, a tomb before the altar of the Holy Cross in Dorchester Abbey had been opened and the remains of Birinus revealed; various miracles had followed. The tomb was re-opened and Archbishop Langton decided that the remains were genuinely those of St Birinus.[21] So began a period of prosperity for, and pilgrimage to, the abbey.

The initial thirteenth-century rebuilding (Fig. 24.3) involved extending the north transept eastwards by adding two chapels, separated from the transept by a two-bay Early English arcade. A date of *c*.1230–50 seems likely, judging by the appearance of the surviving (southern) of the two arches, the northern one, together with the chapel to which it led, having been demolished after the Reformation (Fig. 24.10). The thirteenth-century work appears to have been linked to the creation of the 'more worthy' place for the veneration of St Birinus. Corresponding chapels may have been added to the south transept at this time.

Next, the southern of the two recently built chapels was extended east by three bays, forming the north chancel aisle now known as St Birinus Chapel (Fig. 24.4). The work appears to date from *c*.1250–60. Again, parallel work on the south side

of the chancel may have been done. Finally, in this area of the church, in *c*.1270–80 the walls of the new north chancel aisle were heightened and the present, longer arcade between it and the chancel built (Fig. 24.5). The oldest piece of stained glass in the church, the roundel bearing the name 'Bernius' (*sic*), dates from *c*.1250, and is now in the east window of the north chancel aisle. The west tower was also added, probably at the end of the thirteenth century. Only the stair turret survived the rebuilding of the tower in 1602.

Some of the abbey's principal monuments begin to appear from this period, indicative of the influential supporters or donors who were being attracted. Notable amongst them is the powerful limestone effigy of a knight, dressed in hauberk and coif, legs crossed, turning, with his right hand grasping a sheathed sword, and a lion at his feet. This fine sculpture, with its vivid feeling of movement and strength, was originally in the chancel and was moved by Scott to the south chancel aisle during nineteenth-century restorations. The effigy has been identified[22] as William de Valence, who died in 1282. Also from the late thirteenth or early fourteenth century is the effigy of a Saxon bishop, identified by Leland as Aeschwyn (Aescwig), and probably one of several effigies commissioned to adorn the choir or shrine area

25. *This outstanding sculpture, now in the south chancel aisle, is believed to represent William de Valence, who died in 1282*

and intended to recall Dorchester's impressive episcopal past.[23] The abbey's greatest glories and architectural accomplishments came in the early fourteenth century, when building works must have been under way for over fifty years. In 1292 the momentum was boosted by the granting of indulgences to all who visited the abbey.[24] The sale of indulgences, which were supposed to shorten one's time in purgatory, was widely used by the medieval church for fund-raising. Further grants followed; that of Bishop Dalderby in 1301 offered forty days indulgence to those visiting Birinus's bones. The chronicler Ranulph Higden describes the construction, in c.1320, of a magnificent new shrine to the saint.[25] It was in the south chancel aisle. The present, replica shrine of 1964 is on approximately the same spot. It was in this area that most building was concentrated between the 1290s and 1320s.

The present south chancel arcade, similar to that recently built on the north but with a shortened eastern bay to accommodate the elaborate double-basined piscina for the then high altar, probably dates from the 1290s. At the same time a pair of vaulted chapels to the south east of the south chancel aisle was added. In their east windows was unusual 'split-cusp' tracery, and above them was an upper chapel reached by a stair in the south-east buttresses (Fig. 24.6).

Further improvements soon followed (c.1310–20). To link the new south-east chapels to the south transept, the east wall of the transept was taken down and the south wall extended east, lit by large matching windows separated by buttresses, atop which are carved figures, including men, bears and winged creatures – all distinctly secular. Inside, a more spacious setting had been created for the new shrine of St Birinus (Fig. 24.7). The shrine was of limestone and Purbeck marble, with an intricate vaulted canopy, which had been painted and gilded. The canopy was dismantled at the Reformation, but fragments were

26. This effigy of a Saxon bishop, long identified as Aescwig (c.977–1002), in fact dates from the late 13th or early 14th century, when the abbey was seeking to invoke earlier glories and status

recovered, having been used to block the west door of the north transept. Public access to the shrine could be gained, without disrupting services in the monastic choir, through the small, fourteenth-century door in the west wall. This does, however, seem a disconcertingly modest entrance to so grand a place.

The final phase of the east-end building programme was the extension by one bay of the chancel, creating a new sanctuary (Fig. 24.8). The east end, with its rich and inventive unification of stonework and glass in a single pictorial scheme, is an architectural work of national importance. There is no documentary evidence to reveal the

27. Man and bear, carved atop a buttress to the south chancel aisle, built in c.1310–20 to accommodate the new shrine to St Birinus

name of the master mason or confirm its building dates. Expert opinion puts the work at *c.*1330–40.[26] It was carried out in an unusually sumptuous late, or curvilinear, Decorated style, seen above all in the windows, especially the north window, the tracery of which is in the form of a Tree of Jesse (see illustration on p. 108), and the huge east window, which is entirely filled with reticulated tracery – a unique arrangement. There is abundant ballflower ornament. The effect was further enhanced by the final addition of a canopied piscina and sedilia (the sill of the south window cut away to accommodate them), with gabled, traceried and crocketed heads incorporating figures of saints, and four crocketed spirelets and small rib vaults. To the rear of the sedilia the wall is pierced by small windows in the shape of rounded, cusped triangles, framed with ballflowers – an unconventional and impressive composition.

The research of Tim Ayers has elucidated the complex and sophisticated iconography of the sculpture and stained glass, despite the loss or reworking of some features.[27] The new sanctuary was built on made-up ground above the flood-plain of the River Thame. This, and the ambitious size and construction of the east window, required the insertion of the central buttress rising up through its centre, which reduced the bays of glass from seven to six. The window was further damaged by the post-Reformation lowering of the roof and owes some of its current appearance to nineteenth-century restoration.[28] The east end remains a magnificent sight, both taken together and in detail. The strikingly original Jesse window incorporates stone figures at each intersection, with fragments of linked inscriptions surviving in the glass. The great east window incorporates some original glass and portrays fragments of an Annunciation and Resurrection at the top, Christ in Majesty, the Virgin and Child, symbols of the Trinity and Agnus Dei below, and then a tier of saints, including St Birinus preaching and a donor figure of Ralph Tew, one of the canons. Missing elements in the expected iconographic scheme – for example a Crucifixion sculpture – may be explained by the later intrusion of the buttress.[29] Other donors are thought to be represented by the heraldic glass now in the south window, including the Bigod earls of Norfolk, Edmund Earl of Cornwall, FitzAlan, de Vere, Ferrers, Fitzwalter, Toni, Hastings and Wake. On the transom of the same window stand six stone figures of saints and monks carrying the bier of St Birinus (now broken). It is clear that the work was seen as the culmination of the previous stages of rebuilding, and Ayers has drawn links with contemporary work at major centres such as Oxford, Gloucester and St Albans.

The last major addition to the abbey building was the south aisle, probably in *c.*1350–60 (Fig. 24.9). Rodwell has shown that it was not a parochial aisle, as often assumed, but probably served other functions.[30] A screened private chapel focused on the altar, which was backed by the surviving mid-fourteenth-century wall-painting, and raised up above a substantial crypt or burial vault. The stone-vaulted crypt appears to date from the early fourteenth century and to have had an entrance in the church. There is no clear evidence of an earlier use.[31] High above the altar, but separately aligned to the left, is a shallow pointed recess containing a wall-painting, which Rodwell believes formed the backdrop to a rood, or Christ figure, mounted on a wooden gallery built over the east end of the aisle. The inner part of the aisle would have served as a passage to reach the shrine area and it may be that the gallery and upper chapel were used to display relics to the pilgrims. Thus the new aisle was divided, with separate focuses at upper and lower levels, whilst the original nave continued in parochial use.

By contrast with the great upsurge of religious and building activity at Dorchester in the thirteenth and fourteenth centuries, the period up to the Dissolution of 1536 seems uneventful. The south porch probably dates from the fifteenth century, judging by its outer Perpendicular arch, whilst the guest house appears early sixteenth century (although incorporating reused stonework and a variety of materials). The map of the abbey's properties (see Fig. 20) shows that it was linked to the spiritual and secular life of many places in the area. It was responsible for serving numerous churches and for controlling land and property, ranging from one of the two Dorchester manors, to an estate at Huntercombe, near Nettlebed, to scattered pockets of land elsewhere and to houses in Dorchester and in Oxford (including Brid Hall in Broad Street).[32] The abbey consisted not just of its church and claustral buildings but of a substantial precinct to the north, with barns and agricultural buildings. Anthony Wood wrote in the seventeenth century[33] of 'the great slatted barns, that are supported with buttresses', and these survived to be drawn by John Buckler in the early nineteenth century and, in one case, to be photographed by Henry Taunt in c.1899.

28. One of four ingeniously shaped trefoil windows, surrounded by ballflower ornament and inserted behind the sedilia in the new sanctuary, built c.1340

The life of the abbey and its impact on the adjoining village is tantalizingly underdocumented. One late medieval exception is the reports of visitations undertaken by the bishops of Lincoln in 1441, 1455, 1517 and 1530.[34] These, and the depositions of individual canons giving their views on the conduct of their own house, bring the picture into sharp and often startling focus, showing how closely involved the abbey and the village were. In 1441 the Abbot of Dorchester was John Clifton and there were eleven resident canons. The abbey was £200 in debt, and the abbot had pawned some of its jewels. None of the canons stayed in the cloister after breakfast, but went off hunting and fishing; they ate, drank and played chess in neighbouring taverns; the abbot was alleged to have had five mistresses; meals were rarely eaten in the refectory, but in the abbot's chamber; half the canons were absent looking after their churches. The bishop clamped down. Abbot Clifton was suspended; the abbey clock was to be repaired and hours of service and contemplation strictly kept; the canons were to eat communally; no women were to be admitted to the cloister; and the gates

37

29. Henry Taunt's photograph of c.1899 of a surviving late medieval barn and adjoining cartshed in the former abbey precinct (© Oxfordshire County Council Photographic Archive)

were to be locked at night. These measures were not wholly successful. By 1445, Clifton had been demoted and was one of the seven resident canons (up to half a dozen were absent). Internal tensions (probably meaning that evidence to the bishop lost nothing in the telling) were clear; Ralph Carnelle, a canon, regularly drank with the young canons in the village, carried weapons, and had given the prior so violent a clout on the ear that he was permanently deaf. The bell tower was said to be ruinous, and the annual clothing allowance to canons had been cut from 20s to 13s 4d.

The picture in the final years of the abbey was little better. In 1530 the canons were said to be late risers, often missing matins. One, Thomas Witney, attended church only three times during the year,

spending weeks at his brother's house, and fishing and hunting. The grammar teacher was a drunkard, the buildings out of repair, the cloisters always open as a public thoroughfare, and the monastic church left open to the parish church. This confirms that, within the abbey, the monastic choir, the shrine area, and the parochial nave were clearly separated by screens and gates or doors. These demarcations had obviously lapsed. The bishop again attempted remedies, in particular trying to restrict lay access to the inner precinct and the monastic part of the church, by fitting locks and closing the doors at 5 pm in winter and 6 pm in summer. It was this community – an abbot, prior, six canons and two novices – that would shortly be confronted by the upheavals of Reformation and Dissolution.

Chapter Four

The Dissolution and After: Dorchester Abbey, 1536–*c.*1800

NICHOLAS DOGGETT

30. The church from the south-west, showing the double-ridged south aisle roof, constructed in 1633. Drawing by John Carter, 1792. (The Bodleian Library, University of Oxford, Gough Maps 227, fol. 33)

On 1 October 1534, John March, abbot, with six other canons, Thomas Pyne(r) (? prior), John Clyffton, John Massey, Hugh Landun, George Hart and William Perche, signed the Act of Supremacy.[1] Despite this compliance with Henry VIII's policies, the abbey, as a house with an annual income of less than £200 (it was worth £190 2s 6d per annum in 1535), was suppressed in 1536 under the Act for the Suppression of the Lesser Monasteries.[2] March had become abbot in 1533,[3] succeeding Roger Smith, who (as Bishop Longland's visitation of 1530 had graphically illustrated) had presided over an abbey characterized by secular embroilment, the disrepair of its buildings reflecting the spiritual life of the community.[4]

In November 1536 all the canons except Pyne were granted capacities to 'hold benefices with a complete change of habit' (i.e., to become secular priests).[5] Another Dorchester canon, Thomas

39

Welde (not listed in 1534), had in March that year paid £4 for dispensation to wear the habit of his order beneath that of a secular priest (i.e., to serve as a priest while remaining in the religious life).[6] No canons apparently chose to transfer to another continuing house of the same order, perhaps because they were loath to remain in the religious life, or simply because – of local Augustinian houses – only Osney and Notley, near Thame, continued after 1536.[7] March's only option as abbot was to accept a pension of £22 per annum,[8] payable for life, unless he obtained a royal living, in which case the pension would be extinguished or reduced, depending on the value of the benefice.

It is not known what became of the former Dorchester canons after the Dissolution. The pension commissioners' reports for 1552, 1554 and 1569 do not exist for Oxfordshire. Only that for 1548 survives. It includes the last abbot, who was then dwelling in Dorchester, where he died in April 1553. There is a reference to March's monument on 'a playne marble' in the north chancel aisle in the late seventeenth century,[9] but this no longer survives and it is not known when it was lost. The parish records of churches around Dorchester, particularly the ten parishes which formed the Peculiar,[10] or of those further afield, the advowsons of which had belonged to the abbey before 1536, might reveal the names of former canons as rectors or vicars. Some monasteries were successful in providing for their former brethren in this way, always depending on a vacancy being available and on the importance of the monastic institution involved. A study of the post-Dissolution careers of the ex-religious in Hertfordshire has shown that it was the two wealthiest monastic houses, the Benedictine abbey of St Albans and the college of Bonhommes at Ashridge, which were most successful in obtaining livings for their former members. The smaller houses had less influence.[11] What is clear at Dorchester is that neither of its immediate post-Dissolution vicars, John Matthew (1544–57) and William Edlington (1557–9),[12] had any known connection with the former abbey.

The suppression and the conversion of the church to parochial use

The precise sequence of events at the abbey in the years immediately after 1536 is remarkably unclear. The damage and destruction that occurred at all monasteries must have occurred at Dorchester. The shrine of St Birinus, which as recently as 1535 earned the abbey £5 per annum,[13] must have been broken up at the Dissolution, although intriguingly the grant of the abbey buildings (excluding the church) to Edmund Ashfield of Ewelme in 1544 refers to offerings as 'in decay', rather than entirely absent.[14] Fragments of stonework, almost certainly from the shrine, were discovered in the infill of the west doorway in the north transept during restoration in the 1870s and were eventually incorporated in the shrine reconstruction of 1964.[15] The blocking of the door probably occurred in the seventeenth or eighteenth century, but this should not be taken to imply that the shrine remained intact until then.

Another major loss was the medieval roodloft, the opening to which can still be seen high up in the wall to the east of the south nave arcade. The destruction of this, the setting up of the royal coat of arms in its place, and the covering of wall-paintings with limewash were features of the later phase of religious reforms under Edward VI after 1547. When the Chantry Certificates for Oxfordshire were drawn up at this time, Dorchester had eighty householders. The church had no chantries or chantry priests attached to it.[16] There was one light, supported by land worth 9d per annum. This, and the modest inventory of church goods of 1551–2,[17] again

31. Memorial brass to Abbot Beauforest (d. 1510) and carved choir stall showing his name winding around a crosier, both of them in the chancel, illustrated here by Henry Addington, in 1845 (© Oxfordshire County Council Photographic Archive)

as ordained by Edward VI, suggest a parish and a church which were not wealthy and whose material inheritance from the Middle Ages (the vast abbey building excepted) was not rich.

The medieval Peculiar of Dorchester survived the Dissolution (see also Chapter 6) and, although it is not recorded in the grant of the abbey manor and rectory to Edmund Ashfield in 1544, it continued to descend with them, passing to the Fettiplace family in 1578.[18] John Tregonwell, whose family amassed a fortune from the spoils of the monasteries,[19] was expressing an interest in

the site even before its closure in 1536,[20] but does not seem to have had any involvement after the abbey's suppression. Similarly, while several grants and leases of lands formerly belonging to the abbey occur between 1537 and 1542,[21] there is no further reference to the abbey site itself, until the 1544 grant to Ashfield.

Meanwhile, it is recorded by John Leland, writing in *c.*1542, that the chancel of the former abbey had been bought by Richard Beauforest, a 'great rich man' of Dorchester, for £140 and the whole building made available for parish use.[22]

Leland appears to be the only contemporary source for this and little is known of Beauforest himself, the details of the transaction or why those other parts of the church (long used for parochial worship) were not considered sufficient for the parish. Beauforest's will, made in July 1544 and proved in June 1555, left the whole church to the parish on condition that the parishioners did not sell or change the 'church implements' without the consent of his executors.[23]

Setting aside the whole of a large monastic church for parochial use in this way is unusual. Generally it was that part of the nave used by parishioners before the Dissolution that was pre-served as a parish church.[24] Less often, the eastern part of the church was retained. For example, at the former Augustinian priory of Royston, Hertfordshire, Leland's description strongly sug-gests that the nave was demolished shortly after suppression in 1537. The church there was bought by the townspeople in 1540. There can be little doubt that the acquisition of the whole church would have been a considerable strain on the town's resources and this may have influenced the deci-sion to retain only the eastern end of the church for parochial worship.[25] Other examples of this phenomenon include Abbey Dore (Hereford-shire), Little Malvern, Pershore (Worcestershire) and Boxgrove (Sussex), where the east end was spared largely because of the presence of the mag-nificent de la Warre chantry chapel, completed only in 1535, next to the high altar.[26]

Rarest of all are those former monastic churches, like Dorchester, which were retained almost in their entirety as parish churches. These include Christchurch and Sherborne (Dorset), Romsey (Hampshire), Tewkesbury (Gloucester-shire), St Albans (Hertfordshire), Great Malvern (Worcestershire), Dunster (Somerset) and Cart-mel (Lancashire), all of which survived the Dis-solution substantially intact. The first seven were all in sizeable towns, and at St Albans, where the

medieval parish church abutting the former monastery was demolished after the townspeople bought the abbey church in 1553, there were unfulfilled proposals – first, to make the abbey into a cathedral and then, in Mary's reign, to refound it as a monastery.[27] The preservation of monastic churches at Sherborne and Great Malvern by the townspeople also led to the demolition of parish churches,[28] while at Dunster the monastic church had effectively been taken over by the town even before the Dissolution.[29] At Cartmel it was the chancel and choir (not its short, three-bay nave) which had been used as the parish church, with the whole building retained post-Dissolution.[30]

Why was the whole of the church at Dor-chester, including the nave and south aisle (which were already in non-monastic use), allowed to survive the Dissolution? Dorchester was not a particularly thriving or assertive com-munity in the late 1530s. Unlike Dunster, no dis-putes are recorded over which parts of the monastic church were reserved to the religious and which to the laity. Indeed, with only six or seven canons and the allegations in 1530 that the canons and townspeople moved freely about the church both by night and day, it seems that space within the building was scarcely under pressure. Although Leland refers to three parish churches in Dorchester,[31] this is in the past tense, with no indication that they had recently been demol-ished and certainly not as a direct result of the abbey church becoming a parish church.

Why then did Beauforest feel it necessary to purchase the whole building and why did the townspeople agree to accept his 'gift', a decision that has left generations of parishioners with seri-ous maintenance problems? Beauforest probably had strong family connections with the church. Several antiquarian accounts describe a monu-ment to Richard Bewforest, which in the early eighteenth century stood at the foot of the high

32. The Abbey Guest House, illustrated by J. C. Buckler in 1827

altar on the north side. Thomas Hearne records the inscription coming out of his mouth: *O Dulcis Mater, Virgo Virginum ora pro nobis tuum filium.*[32] The brass remains in this position today, with the rather more Protestant-sounding – but still clearly sixteenth-century – English inscription 'pray ihs geve his sowle good Rest,' (? added) at its foot. It is now accepted[33] that the figure on the brass commemorates Abbot Richard Beauforest (d. 1510). He may well have been a relative of Richard Beauforest, donor of the abbey to Dorchester. Another brass, damaged and relocated from the chancel in *c.*1850, is now set in the floor of the south chancel aisle. It has been identified as that of Margaret Beauforest and her two husbands, William Tanner and Richard Beauforest, donor of the church (see illustration on p. 109).[34] This is certainly not the grand monument of one seeking to make the whole church a reminder of his importance.

It is tempting to speculate that the entire church was preserved because it was considered, albeit briefly, as a potential cathedral for the new diocese of Oxford, a role allocated in the event to Osney (from 1542) and then Christ Church (from 1546).[35] Or perhaps Beauforest and his fel-

low parishioners acted out of attachment to the great building in their midst?

It is unlikely that Beauforest's motivation (or that of others) will ever be clear, although his bequest of only twenty shillings to 'Reparations of my Parishe Church' suggests that he may not have fully considered the long-term implications for the parish.[36] It is known that his interest was limited to the church, which was excluded from the grant of the rest of the site to Ashfield in 1544.

The cloister and other buildings

The 1544 grant reveals no details of the buildings acquired by Ashfield, which presumably included those around the cloister. The lack of later documentary references to the domestic buildings suggests that, with the exception of the abbey guest house, they may have been quickly demolished. Certainly, destruction at Dorchester was exceptionally complete.

Other than the guest house, no building appears to have survived to be recorded by Anthony Wood in 1657, although Rodwell has recently suggested[37] that Edmund Ashfield may have created a manorial seat in the former monastic buildings immediately to the north-west of the church. The enclosed passage recorded by Wood alongside the north wall and leading into the north aisle would, in this interpretation, have led to a private family pew. Such adaptive reuse of many monastic sites of similar size and importance to Dorchester was widespread between 1540 and 1600.[38] However, the abbey manor passed to the Fettiplace family, with their extensive estates elsewhere, in 1578. This and the fact that extensive antiquarian interest in Dorchester from this period onwards would surely have documented the survival of any significant remains beyond c.1600 suggest that Dorchester's monastic buildings disappeared relatively early.

Wood's plan of the church, closely followed by several later antiquaries,[39] is clearly not to scale and is of use primarily for the evidence it provides of the enclosed walk remaining on the north side of the nave already mentioned. To the north and west of the church the plan also marks 'The Court within the Abbey', into which lead two doors in the stretch of wall immediately west of the tower. It was in this area that in 1657 Wood wrote that '. . . in digging at the west end of the church there was discovered a small vault that would hold 3 or 4 men or more, and at the top was a tonnell, like unto a chimney but something larger [which] when the abbey was standing . . . did go to the uppermost rooms.'[40]

The church in the seventeenth century and the visit of William Stukeley in 1736

The costly building of a new western tower was undertaken in 1602, replacing the medieval tower, of which only the stair turret at the south-east angle survived the rebuilding.[41] Perhaps the work was a consequence of demolition and reordering in the area of the gatehouse, which is believed to have linked the west end of the church and the guest house. The 1602 rebuilding may not, however, have been as extensive as is sometimes thought. That work occurred is undeniable from the carved initials 'JW' and the date '1602' near the top of the south-west buttress and the reference in the parish registers to 'The tower of Dorchester rebuilt by J.W. 1602,' but both may relate to no more than remodelling. Certainly the appearance of the tower is completely traditional in character, with its flint and stone chequer-work turrets, Y-tracery windows of thirteenth-century style in the top stage and battlemented parapet. Without the evidence to the contrary, the tower would probably be dated on stylistic grounds to c.1500, but Wood's 1657 statement is clear: 'the tower that now is, is but of late standing, the staircase old.'[42] A new bell was added to the two original bells in the tower in 1591 and three more were hung in 1603, 1606 and 1651.[43] There was also a chiming clock by the 1620s.[44]

The maintenance of such a large building proved a considerable burden on the churchwardens and parishioners, and there are complaints in the visitation returns about its poor condition, both the chancel and the nave being reported as neglected in the 1620s.[45] The records of the Peculiar court at this time show persistent resistance to the payment of church dues, both by Dorchester parishioners and by adjoining parishes with continuing obligations to the mother church of the jurisdiction. Non-payment increasingly reflected religious nonconformity, both by Roman Catholics and Protestant dissenters, amongst them some of Dorchester's leading families. This new religious climate affected both the fabric and the standing of the abbey in the local community, on which it was now much more closely dependent. The links between church and community are further explored in Chapter 6.

Limited resources were probably the reason for

33. The church from the north-west in 1809, showing the hip-roofed structure at the west end of the nave. Watercolour by J. C. Buckler (The Bodleian Library, University of Oxford, MS. Top. Oxon. d. 66, no. 218)

demolishing the northern half of the north transept, the truncated remains of which were then incorporated into an extended north chancel aisle by means of a roughly built wall sealing the gap, with a new, four-light window in spindly 'Churchwarden Gothic' style inserted in the north wall (see Fig. II, on p. 102). The thirteenth-century east chapel of the north transept was also removed at this time, although part of the piscina from the east wall of this chapel still survives in a recess in the north chancel aisle.[46] Otherwise, the seventeenth century was largely a period of patching and remodelling existing fabric. In 1633 the original roof of the south aisle was replaced by a

double-ridged construction,[47] the valley of the new roof breaking through the arch of the west window, which was filled in as a result. The porch roof also seems to have been raised at the same time, blocking part of the window behind it. Virtually nothing is known about the church's appearance during the Commonwealth, other than Wood's statement that some of the glass figures in the Jesse window had been broken by Parliamentarian soldiers during the Civil War.[48]

A seventeenth-century date has sometimes been attributed to the two rather crude round-headed arches on the north and south sides of the crossing. Cutting the twelfth-century string

45

course, they are clearly not Anglo-Saxon as was once thought.[49] In this connection a previously unpublished manuscript account of a visit by the famous antiquary William Stukeley on 1 September 1736 is worth quoting. After stating that 'the whole cathedral seems to consist of two churches at least, join'd together' and that he considered the older parts of the church to be on the south and west, Stukeley wrote:

> there are 2 semicircular arches on the n. & on the s. of the middle isle in that part wch may be calld the nave or cross isle of the original work of Birinus . . . There are many antient monuments of bishops & religious & some of antient nobility etc Most flat on the ground the brasses mostly taken away much of the oldest small paving tyles colored with figures & laid mosaic with wch the whole quire was pavd some of the altar part within railes yet undisturbd & in little triangular bits with borders. much painted glass extremely antient & of Saxon times & letters, in the window s. of high altar st. pet crucyfyd with head downwards. st. paul beheaded . . .'[50]

Stukeley may have failed to notice that the arches cut through the Norman string-course, or not have understood the significance of this. But even in this case, the arches would surely have been recognizable as relatively new features at this time, rather than appearing as 'the original work of Birinus'. This poses the interesting possibility that when Stukeley visited, the arches were narrower than they are today and still sat beneath the string-course, although anyone not disposed to accept this suggestion could reasonably point to the unsupported nature of another of Stukeley's conclusions, that the older parts of the church lay to the south. An intensive architectural survey by Warwick Rodwell (2005) concluded that there were, indeed, no tall, open

34. Later arch cutting through the 12th-century string-course on the south side of the crossing

lateral arches in the crossing of the late twelfth-century abbey and dates the present arches to the later Middle Ages, when the rebuilding of the chancel destroyed the east side of an existing crossing (see p. 32).

Remodelling and repair in the eighteenth century

Shortly after Stukeley's visit a series of changes to the fabric followed the submission of estimates for repairs costing £2,500 in 1737. Although only £714 was raised, in 1739 carpenters from Oxford and London were instructed to repair the roof of the south chancel aisle and a plumber engaged to cover it with lead,[51] it presumably being at this time that the flat plastered ceiling (itself removed in 1872–4) replaced the original medieval vaulting. In 1746 the chancel was refurbished at the expense of the Fettiplace family, the owner of the great tithes, the work including the erection of a classical altarpiece, the insertion of another flat plaster ceiling (which cut across the head of the great east window) and the repaving of the floor, during which several tombs were discovered.[52] The west end of the nave was

Dorchester Ch. Oxon Augt 14 1824

35. *The crowded east end in the early 19th century. Pencil drawing by John Preston Neale on 14 August 1824, showing the auditory layout with three-decker pulpit, box pews and the classical reredos installed in 1745. (The Bodleian Library, University of Oxford, MS. Top. Oxon. b. 283, fol. 12)*

47

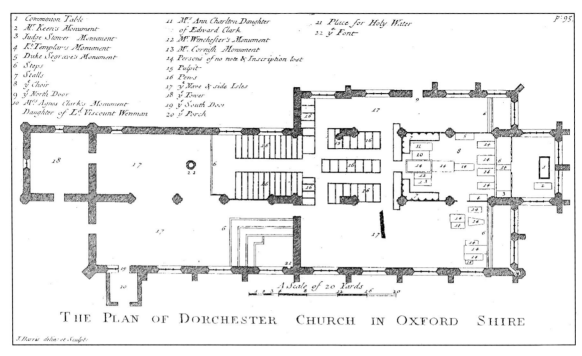

1. Communion Table
2. Mr Keen's Monument
3. Judge Stower Monument
4. Kt Templar's Monument
5. Duke Segrave's Monument
6. Steps
7. Stalls
8. ye Choir
9. ye North Door
10. Mrs Agnes Clarkes Monument Daughter of Lt Viscount Wenman

11. Mrs Ann Charlton Daughter of Edward Clark
12. Mr Winchester's Monument
13. Mr Cornish Monument
14. Persons of no note & Inscription lost
15. Pulpit
16. Pews
17. ye Nave & side Isles
18. ye Tower
19. ye South Door
20. ye Porch

21. Place for Holy Water
22. ye Font

P: 95.

A Scale of 20 Yards

THE PLAN OF DORCHESTER CHURCH IN OXFORD SHIRE

J. Harris delin: et Sculpt:

36. Plan of the abbey drawn by J. Harris in 1722 for the amplified edition of Dugdale's 'Monasticon', published by John Stevens in the following year. The plan shows the post-Reformation layout of the abbey interior for Anglican worship in the auditory style. It has strong similarities with plans by John Carter (1792–3) and Henry Hinton (1807).

repaved in 1747 and the north aisle in 1765.[53] The eighteenth-century interior of the church, with a Jacobean pulpit, box pews and communion rail, is usefully shown in a pencil drawing by John Preston Neale of 1824 and there is a plan of the church, apparently drawn by Henry Hinton in 1807.[54] These are just two amongst a rich array of drawings, plans and notes of the abbey, produced by a succession of antiquaries starting with John Carter in 1792–3. His proposed *Antiquities of Dorchester* was never in fact published, although the fine and informative drawings survive. In succeeding years investigation became ever more enthusiastic, along with increasing calls for restoration, as the next chapter of the abbey's history shows.

Chapter Five

The Abbey Restored, *c.*1800–1920

GEOFFREY TYACK

Dorchester Abbey at the end of the eighteenth century was in a dilapidated but, for a large medieval monastic church in a poor rural parish, surprisingly intact condition. The main damage since the Reformation had been the destruction of the north transept and its eastern chapel. The fourteenth-century stone vault had also been removed from the south chancel chapel, the original wooden roofs replaced throughout the church and, worst of all from a visual point of view, the upper part of the east window truncated in the 1740s following the insertion of a plaster ceiling over the chancel and sanctuary. Much of the magnificent fourteenth-century sculpture in the sanctuary was also damaged, but not irreparably. The assortment of roof lines and blocked windows bore witness to spasmodic and makeshift repairs or work left undone and, judging from Skelton's view from the south-east in 1823, parapets and turrets had already crumbled as bushes sprouted from the walls.

The interior was laid out for the performance of Anglican worship according to the rubrics of the 1662 Book of Common Prayer. At points during the late eighteenth century, the court of the Dorchester Peculiar[1] had granted faculties

37. The abbey was in a ruinous state by the early 19th century, as seen here in an engraving for Skelton's 'Antiquities of Oxfordshire' (1823)

allowing various individuals to extend and remake their personal family pews in the abbey, creating a jumble of old seats and new box pews of varying heights, which finally led, in 1792, to a wholesale rationalization of the abbey's pews. Appropriated and numbered pews were now carefully allocated to specified persons, with some left 'to be resorted to in common as formerly'. This arrangement remained essentially intact until the first Victorian restoration of the late 1840s.

The layout is captured in a contemporary plan (Fig. 36).[2] Seats were grouped in an aligned layout of box pews, focused on a pulpit with sounding board, elevated above a reading desk and placed against the north-eastern pier of the former crossing. Most of the services were conducted from here, and not from the sanctuary, which was only used during the infrequent celebrations of Holy Communion. The rest of the church – the nave, the spacious south aisle, the south chancel aisle (the former site of St Birinus's shrine) and the north chancel aisle – were largely empty and unused. The east end and sanctuary were seemingly empty too. The plan shows a communion table and a single tomb, 'of Mr Keen'. Skelton's interior view[3] is even more stark, with no altar, furnishings or choir-stalls in an east end over which a lowered, plastered ceiling presses, obscuring the top of the great east window.

The work of other contemporary illustrators throws doubt on this apparent total emptiness.[4] Amongst them, Britton's *Chronological History of English Architecture* (1821) shows a draped table, with books and chairs. Most convincing of all is perhaps the delicately detailed and precisely dated pencil drawing of the interior of the abbey, made by Neale on 14 August 1824 (Fig. 35).[5] This shows an eighteenth-century wooden reredos against the east wall, with a central pediment and panels bearing texts, consistent in style with the date of 1746 for the erection of an altarpiece and

the repaving of the chancel referred to in another description of 1807.[6] In front was an altar rail, then an area with the remnants of the fifteenth-century stalls facing inwards, and separated from the massed box pews by a low screen, through which parishioners would 'draw near in faith' at the appropriate point of the Communion service. On the northern side of the pewed area was the Jacobean-style, three decker pulpit.[7] The 'working' part of the church was screened off from the nave, in the middle of which stood the medieval font.

The first person to call for the restoration of the abbey was the antiquary John Carter.[8] Not long afterwards, the ubiquitous John Buckler, surveyor of Magdalen College, Oxford, and one of the greatest of all Oxford topographical artists, produced, together with his son John Chessell Buckler, a detailed and accurate visual record of the state of the fabric in a series of pencil drawings and watercolours (Fig. 33).[9] The accurate recording of a historic fabric is an essential step towards its restoration – or, to use a less loaded word, conservation. But at Dorchester this could not occur without adequate funding. As a Peculiar until *c*.1837, the church was described as an 'ecclesiastical oasis'.[10] Following the sale of the abbey manor by the Fettiplace family in 1808, the tithes were leased by the Roman Catholic Davey family. They were legally bound to pay for essential repairs to the chancel, but had no obligation to fund a more thorough restoration; the rest of the church was the responsibility of the parishioners.[11] Church rates could not be relied upon to fund extensive repairs, though they were later used to supplement other sources of income.[12] Some changes were nevertheless carried out in 1806–7, when a long-standing local inhabitant, Colonel Kennett, 'personally attended the removal of the scattered fragments [of medieval stained glass] which were in the different windows of the church, and had them carefully and tastefully arranged in the windows of the chancel'.[13] The medieval glass in the sanctuary windows still remains as he left it, to the confusion of those trying to reconstruct the original iconography of the east end of the church.[14] Then in 1809 the font was removed from the nave to the south chancel chapel and the screen, or 'west gallery' as it was called, blocking off the chancel from the nave, removed in order to open up a vista through the church.[15]

For the first four decades of the nineteenth century Dorchester was served by non-resident clergy – technically, perpetual curates – who delegated their duties to poorly paid deputies.[16] In

38. The interior of the chancel, portrayed in a suspiciously empty state, in Britton's 'Chronological History of English Architecture' (1835)

1838, however, the patron of the living, General Burrows, appointed a new incumbent, Richard Walker. Following soon after the launching of the Oxford Movement in 1833, this presaged both a revival of parish life and a renewed interest in the history of the building, which bore fruit in the publication of the first printed history of the church in 1845.[17] Meanwhile, in September 1844, an Oxford architect, James Cranston,[18] was commissioned by the Oxford Architectural (now the Architectural and Historical) Society (hereafter OAS) to produce a report on the state of the fabric. The Society – whose members included the bookseller and antiquarian J. H. Parker, the medieval historian E. A. Freeman and the young John Ruskin – had been founded in 1839 'for promoting the study of Gothic architecture': an aim furthered through meetings, lectures and publications.[19] Though less combative, and less bigoted, than the better-known Cambridge Camden Society, it sought to influence contemporary taste through a better understanding of medieval architecture, and saw Dorchester Abbey as an opportunity to promote a 'model restoration' of a major medieval church not far from Oxford. The Society could help fund this work by appeals to its members and, by influencing the character of the restoration, could help set standards that might be applicable elsewhere.

In his report Cranston said that the abbey had suffered greatly from neglect and natural decay, and that some parts were unsound and dilapidated.[20] He drew attention to the loss of all the medieval roofs, the division of the nave by plaster partitions and the poor state of the chancel and sanctuary. Here, quite apart from the destruction of the upper part of the east window, much of the fourteenth-century carving had been lost or broken and the lead of the windows allowed to decay to the point where the stained glass was at risk. Nevertheless, enough of the original work survived to make a restoration along what Freeman called 'strictly conservative' principles feasible.[21] Remains of the stone reredos lay behind the eighteenth-century wooden reredos, the medieval corbels of the lost nave roof survived, and there was enough evidence to enable the reconstruction of the upper part of the east window, the stair turret at the east end and the buttress at the west end of the south aisle, the roof of the porch and sundry other repairs and improvements. Together with the replacement of all the roofs – by far the most expensive item – the cost of a complete restoration was estimated at £3,970 (estimated equivalent in 2003 values £305,000).

This sum was clearly too much for a poor parish to raise all at once, even with the help of the OAS, and Cranston recommended starting work on the chancel, the part of the church in most desperate need of repair. A contract was therefore drawn up on 30 October 1845 for the repair of the sedilia, piscina and south window of the sanctuary 'in the spirit of the old work' at a cost of £130.[22] This involved taking down and replacing the tracery without the iron bars that had prevented it from leaning outwards.[23] The project was funded by a monthly offertory from the parishioners over a period of eight months and by contributions from parishioners including the Daveys, who later paid for the elegant Roman Catholic church of St Birinus at Bridge End.[24] Cranston was architect of the work at the abbey and John Castle, of Cowley Road, Oxford, builder.[25]

As the work on the sedilia and south window neared completion, the OAS issued an appeal on 12 February 1846 to the 'many persons interested in Ecclesiastical Architecture' for funding to enable the north and east windows to be restored while the scaffolding was still in place, and on 20 March 1846 another contract for £38 was issued to Cranston and Castle for repairing the north (Jesse) window. The appeal brought in

39. *William Butterfield, known for his devout adherence to the principles of the Oxford Movement, was architect for the restorations at Dorchester from 1847 to 1858. His transformation of the east end and its fittings is shown here.*

£501, and the OAS turned to one of its members, James Park Harrison, to prepare designs for the restoration of the east window in place of Cranston, whose proposals were deemed too elaborate.[26] This most ambitious project to date involved not only the re-creation of the upper part of the window with its stone 'wheel' of tracery but also the construction of a new sanctuary roof. But soon after supplying designs, Harrison, who had a private income, resigned because the Society could not accept his insistence that the work be done without payment.[27] The work was then entrusted to the 32-year-old William Butterfield.

Butterfield is best known today as the creator and arguably the most gifted exponent of the startlingly original 'High Victorian' Gothic style of architecture, first launched with the Ecclesiological Society's 'model church' of All

40. Butterfield's brightly coloured tiles can still be seen on the east wall, behind Scott's unfinished reredos of 1875

Saints, Margaret Street, London, in 1849. But in the earlier stages of his career his architecture was more restrained, owing something to the example of that prophet of Victorian Gothic A. W. N. Pugin, something to his devout adherence to the principles of the Oxford Movement, and something too to his own understanding of medieval and vernacular building techniques. Since 1843 he had been employed by Benjamin Webb, one of the leading lights of the Cambridge Camden (later Ecclesiological) Society – in many ways the architectural wing of the Oxford Movement – to prepare model designs for church fittings to help the growing numbers of clergy and architects involved in restoring medieval churches.[28] These designs were published as *Instrumenta Ecclesiastica* between 1844 and 1847, and, partly through Webb's friend Alexander Beresford Hope – a contributor to the Dorchester Abbey appeal – he gained a number of important architectural commissions, for new churches, church schools, and, in 1844, for St Augustine's theological college in Canterbury.[29] He also became involved in several schemes of restoration, including those of the great fourteenth-century church of Ottery St Mary, Devon, and the late-thirteenth-century chapel of Merton College, Oxford, the latter carried out with great sensitivity to the original fabric – though with almost complete disregard of the aesthetic virtues of later interventions – in 1849–56. At Dorchester Abbey the post-medieval work was, whatever its historical value, of minimal aesthetic interest, and only the most doctrinaire conservationist would now question the fact that Butterfield enhanced the beauty of what is both liturgically and historically the most important part of the building.

The most prominent feature of Butterfield's restoration was the upper part of the east window, with its traceried rose of elaborate ogee-patterned tracery characteristic of English late Decorated or even French Flamboyant work, carved in 1846–7 by G. P. White, of Vauxhall Bridge Road, Westminster.[30] James Park Harrison had already discovered limited remnants of the original fourteenth-century tracery,[31] but the upper part of the window now is effectively Butterfield's, including what E. A. Freeman called the 'freakish' arrangement whereby the upper part of the circle flows into the pointed arch.[32] Also Butterfield's is the splendid steeply pitched arch-braced wooden sanctuary roof that replaced the previous flat plaster ceiling. Architectural restoration was accompanied in 1847 by a refurbishment of the sanctuary to make it suitable for regular celebrations of the Eucharist – now, in the aftermath of the Oxford Movement, a central and growing part of Anglican liturgical practice. A new raised floor was therefore supplied, paved with encaustic tiles, and behind a new, stone-topped altar against the east wall Butterfield designed a splendid alabaster reredos – now alas hidden – with tessellated blue, white and red tiles and a red marble cross.[33] Stained glass in the new upper roundel of the east window, showing Christ in Majesty attended by angels, was supplied by Michael O'Connor, a pupil of Thomas Willement,[34] using funds raised at Oriel College, Oxford, that nursery of the Oxford Movement; new glass in the south sanctuary window was by Pugin's associate, John Hardman, and other glass by James Powell, a prolific early Victorian stained-glass manufacturer.[35] John Thomas, possibly the man who did much of the sculpture at the new Houses of Parliament, was paid £7 10s for figures of St Peter and St Paul.[36] By spring 1847 the OAS reported that the east end of the sanctuary had been 'restored to its original magnificence' and the east window returned to its 'primitive grandeur'. After a hiatus due to an interruption in funding, the roof was completed in 1850.[37]

By now the OAS funds had completely run out, largely because of the cost of the oak tim-

41. Butterfield's pulpit of 1852–3, restored to a position in the chancel in 2000

bers of Butterfield's new roof. Work halted until 1852–3, when, with money once more available from a fund established by the incumbent, William Addison, Butterfield turned to the refurbishment of the former monastic choir.[38] This involved replacing or drastically refashioning the existing furnishings and flooring, and the removal and resiting of the medieval tombs in the south chancel aisle.[39] In a letter apparently to the recently established Oxford Diocesan Church Building Society, Addison pointed out that there were only 320 seats in the church for a population of over 1000 people, and that none of the seats were free for use by the poor, save for 140 Sunday-school children who sat on benches. In place of the earlier private box pews

Butterfield designed 'free and open' pews for 530 people, along with seating for 185 children, thus making the church more accessible to a growing population in need of evangelization – a major aim of the Oxford Movement.[40] The new pews replaced the old box pews in the crossing and the western part of the monastic choir and were separated from the eastern bays of the chancel by a new wooden screen (since removed), next to which was a wooden pulpit embellished with cusped arches surmounted by trefoils, also designed by Butterfield, and recently restored. To the east of the screen Butterfield supplied inward-facing choir-stalls and wooden screens to the north and south chancel aisles, all incorporating existing woodwork; the eastern bay, next to the sanctuary, was left free of furnishings, except for kneelers and book rests, to which, in a survival of earlier practice, 'all communicants [proceeded] from their seats in the nave at the commencement of the communion service'.[41] New floors of York stone and encaustic tiles were introduced, the wooden roof of the sanctuary extended two bays westwards and the ancient lead font put on a new stone base more appropriate to its twelfth-century date.[42]

The cost of the work was £2,000, and in 1854 the often hypercritical *Ecclesiologist* praised Butterfield for his 'bold and masterly' restoration, although criticizing him for making the chancel screen too high and solid, and for gluing corbels on to the pulpit, an offence against the Puginian gospel of 'honesty'.[43] Butterfield responded vigorously, reminding readers that the screen was no higher than the previous one, that it incorporated valuable old woodwork and that he did not wish to 'adapt [it] or drag [it] down to the level of a village congregation or service ... The thing to be done under the circumstances certainly was to copy and restore.' He also expressed the hope that the church might eventually become attached to a college or even become a tempo-rary cathedral.[44] As for the pulpit: 'I have simply used, visibly, that sort of work which is concealed, more or less, in most joiners' work.'[45] Seen after an interval of 150 years, Butterfield's reordering of the monastic choir appears a thoughtful and aesthetically effective response to the liturgical needs of the period. Fortunately recent restoration work has reversed much of the damaging effect of later meddling, inspired by an all-too-common twentieth-century reaction against Victorian art and architecture.

In 1856 William Addison resigned the living. He was replaced by W. C. Macfarlane, who carried the restoration of the abbey forward to completion. Described in his obituary (1885) as 'one of the staunchest supporters of the High Church party', he instituted choral services and devoted much of his private fortune to the parish.[46] But first he commissioned a large and impressive new vicarage to replace the rented house in which his predecessor had been obliged to live.[47] Here he lived with his unmarried sister, epitomizing the Oxford Movement ideal of a resident parson – an essential complement of church restoration as it was conceived by the Victorians.

Before Macfarlane became incumbent, Butterfield had provided plans – now, alas, lost – for the restoration of the rest of the church and working drawings for the north aisle. But largely through Macfarlane's influence, he was now dropped as architect in favour of another luminary of Victorian church architecture: George Gilbert Scott.[48] Three years older than Butterfield, Scott had been involved in the ecclesiologically 'correct' restoration of medieval churches since the early 1840s, when, after coming into contact with the Cambridge Camden Society and reading some of Pugin's polemical writings, he had found himself 'like a person awakened from a long feverish dream'.[49] Like Butterfield and most of his contemporaries, he

42. The new vicarage, built for William Macfarlane at the beginning of his long incumbency in 1856. He became the first resident parson for some seventy years. (Photograph of 1907, © Oxfordshire County Council Photographic Archive)

had no compunction in removing 'inappropriate' later work in order to reveal the original character of a medieval church, especially if it was, like Dorchester, of the favoured 'Middle Pointed' (Decorated) period of Gothic architecture. This sometimes led him into what the zealots of the younger generation, inspired by Ruskin and led by William Morris, later condemned as totally unwarranted destruction, as dangerous as anything carried out by the long-vilified James Wyatt. However, at Dorchester Abbey, as in many of the large number of churches he restored throughout the country, Scott was content to abide by the 'conservative'

principles adumbrated by the OAS when it first took an interest in the building in 1844.

Scott's first task was to restore the north chancel aisle, including a new wooden lean-to roof, a project carried out in 1859 using voluntary subscriptions and funds held over by the OAS until the reroofing of the choir had been completed.[50] In 1860 the east end of the chancel was underpinned, and in 1861 the low double-pitched roof of the 1630s over the south aisle was replaced by the present single-span crown-post wooden roof at a cost of £894, chiefly supplied by subscriptions, Macfarlane himself contributing £226. The porch was reroofed, the lower pitch

57

43. George Gilbert Scott's proposed restoration of the south chancel aisle and chapels, including the re-creation of the lost stone vaulting. This, and much other work, was carried out during Scott's time as architect at Dorchester (1858–78).

enabling the window above to be properly seen, and Scott also designed the wooden inner porch – recently removed – to keep out draughts.[51] The nave was tackled next, in 1862, when a new roof, also of the crown-post type, was erected at a cost of £800 (over half of which was contributed by Macfarlane). This left only the west bay of the monastic choir and the crossing to be reroofed and, after this had been done for £1,210 in 1863, Macfarlane could record in the back of a school

register, where he noted progress, that 'the whole church was . . . thrown open.' The high altar could now be seen from the west end of the church, and in 1863 the firm of Clayton and Bell, best known for its stained glass, was paid £65 for painting the lower parts of the chancel walls and for restoring the fourteenth-century wall-painting over the former parochial altar, or farmers' altar, as it was then called;[52] a stove was installed in the nave in 1867.[53] Macfarlane had already supplied new choir stalls at his own expense in 1862, and in 1870–5 an organ, by Walker, was built in the north chancel aisle.[54] Choral services with a surpliced choir and organ accompaniment were now possible – something regarded as timeless by many modern Anglicans, but, like so much in the modern Church of England, largely, so far as parish churches are concerned, an invention of the Victorian period.

Attention now shifted to the tower. This was repaired in 1868–9 at a cost of £1,100 under the direction of J. M. Bignell, one of Scott's pupils, the approach to the church having already been beautified by the erection in 1867 of the distinctive lych-gate, almost certainly designed by Scott and funded by George May of Dedworth House, near Reading, in memory of his wife.[55] The only part of the church that now remained unrestored was the south chancel aisle, for which another fund-raising campaign was launched, this time for £1,637. The aisle roof was tackled by Scott in 1872, and at the same time the sharply pointed turret to the staircase at the south-east corner was added to his designs; two years later, in 1874, the ribbed vaults to the eastern chapels were added, 'there being enough indication of the old work for Mr Bignell to complete the design.'[56] They were suitably refurbished with stained glass of the Ascension (north chapel) and the Resurrection (south chapel) by Hardman; the north chapel was further embellished with paintings of the Annunciation and an

44. The east end, c.1890, laid out for High Church worship, with an enclosed area for the choir and, beyond, a raised altar with candlesticks (© Oxfordshire County Council Photographic Archive)

altar in memory of Samuel Wilberforce ('Soapy Sam'), Bishop of Oxford from 1845 to 1869. The stained glass in the two eastern windows of the south wall was inserted in 1899 to the somewhat sentimental designs of Mayer of Munich.

Macfarlane was also responsible for removing Butterfield's screen and raising the altar in the sanctuary to its present height – a reflection, no doubt, of his 'advanced' high-church sentiments. The present reredos was designed by John Medland, another of Scott's pupils, unfortunately hiding Butterfield's reredos, and at about the same time new glass for the two lower rows of lights of the east window was supplied by

Clayton and Bell.[57] Scott died in 1878, having also designed an attractive new parochial school of brick (1871–2) and suggested adaptations in 1877–8 of existing houses in Queen Street for a missionary college, thus echoing Butterfield's suggestion that the abbey might become a collegiate church; the tile-hung façade is still an embellishment to the High Street.[58] And it was Scott's pupil Bignell who supplied the designs in 1883 for the west window of the old parochial aisle, the final work of restoration.[59] Two years later Macfarlane himself was dead.

By the 1880s the word restoration had acquired negative connotations that it has never entirely shaken off, at least when applied to medieval churches. Restoration, fulminated John Ruskin, was 'a lie from beginning to end'. For his disciple William Morris, alterations to historic buildings were part of the history of those buildings, and the removal of such alterations, especially in the interests of taking a building back to an imagined state of pristine purity, amounted to a gratuitous destruction of its history and, by extension, that of the community of which it formed a part. Nowadays, by a strange paradox, conservationists can be equally vehement in the defence of those very Victorian alterations to historic churches that Morris and his Society for the Protection of Ancient Buildings so loathed. For, in the process of restoring churches, the Victorians often not only rescued many of them from neglect and decrepitude but also enhanced their beauty. Such was the case at Dorchester Abbey.

45. *Dorchester High Street in 1904, with the tile-hung buildings of the Missionary College on the left. The college was founded by William Macfarlane in 1878, shortly after restoration of the church was completed. Its clergy and students were to play a major part in the ministry of the abbey until after the First World War. (© Oxfordshire County Council Photographic Archive)*

Chapter Six

Religion and Community: Dorchester to 1920

KATE TILLER

The religious life of Dorchester was transformed between the 1780s and the 1920s in ways which tell us much about the abbey, about other denominations, about Dorchester as a community, and about wider trends in religious and social history. This chapter follows the story from these perspectives, and begins with a brief picture of the local setting for religious change.

Around the abbey lay a predominantly agricultural community, arguably with signs of earlier urban status, but now essentially a large village.[1]

On to this was superimposed a major thoroughfare, the route linking London to Oxford and to Worcester, Gloucester and South Wales, which was turnpiked from 1736 to 1874. At the beginning of our period this thoroughfare was still a major and positive feature in Dorchester's life. In 1813–15 the handsome new bridge was built, and the road, with toll-house and milestone, cut into the south-west of the churchyard. The road brought goods, post, news, ideas, travellers and their business. In 1821 Dorchester had seven

46. Hens frequent the deserted yard of The George Inn, opposite the abbey, in c.1890. The demise of the coaching trade was one factor in Dorchester's dwindling fortunes in the 19th century. (© Oxfordshire County Council Photographic Archive)

licensed inns.[2] When the fortunes of the coaching trade began to dwindle in the 1830s, so did those of Dorchester. There was to be no compensating railway link, the nearest connection being Culham, two miles west, opened in 1844 on the GWR line to Oxford.

The size of population is a telling barometer of the fortunes of a community. That of Dorchester (including its hamlets of Overy and Burcot) was 913 at the first national census in 1801, an estimated doubling in size since the late seventeenth century. This and eighteenth-century parish records point to a growing community and one experiencing increasing hardship, judged by the accelerating levels of poor relief expenditure and employment schemes introduced by the parish vestry from the 1770s.[3] The problem proved endemic. In 1834 twelve per cent of the local population (21 able-bodied men, 16 women, 52 children and 39 infirm) were receiving relief. To this was added the loss of the coaching trade and allied business. By 1811 (after a decade in which many rural Oxfordshire settlements grew markedly), Dorchester had actually fallen in size, to 901. Despite a 'revival' to 999 in 1821, Dorchester's population was then barely sustained, peaking at 1,097 in 1861. Thereafter it declined, falling away to 944 by 1901, little more than at the start of the century.

Dorchester then was a place of diminishing economic diversity and a community under stress. Its agriculture was heavily dependent on arable. In 1840 only about an eighth of the parish acreage of 2,633 was meadow or pasture.[4] During the Swing Riots of 1830 at Burcot, threshing machines (seen as a threat to the valuable winter work of hand threshing) were broken, 'there was huzzaing, blowing of horns, and shouting' and a rioter was heard to say, 'there had been fires and there would be more.'[5] Until its very late parliamentary enclosure in 1861, Dorchester's fields operated under a long-surviving open-field sys-

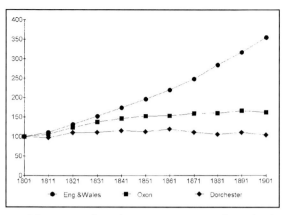

47. A barometer of Dorchester's situation: population levels 1801–1901, compared with county and national trends

tem (although with some earlier enclosures to the west and north of the village). Despite this seemingly archaic setting, some of the largest enterprises were renowned well beyond the locality for their innovation and efficiency, notably the Daveys of Overy and Thomas Latham of Dorchester and neighbouring Clifton, both of whom were highly praised by no less than Arthur Young.[6] He considered 'Mr Davey one of the most intelligent farmers in the county' and enjoined other Oxfordshire gentlemen, 'let them come to Dorchester; they may take a lesson very well worth a long journey.' It was men such as Davey, notable also as a leading Roman Catholic, who were leaders of the Dorchester community. The principal manorial lords, the Berties, earls of Abingdon, and the Fettiplaces were absentee. The Fettiplaces sold up in 1808, with the Daveys amongst those extending their interests as a result. (With their purchase, the Catholic Daveys also acquired the tithe rights associated with responsibility for repair of the abbey chancel, an intriguing situation, even in a place where Anglican and Catholic had coexisted since the Reformation.)

The 1870s were another period of change for Dorchester, with the Davey farm at Overy sold to St John's College, Oxford, in 1874, and the main manorial estate sold by the Berties in 1876. It was at this time, too, that a national depression in agriculture began which lasted out the century. Dorchester felt this badly. Agricultural wages were amongst the lowest in the country. Landholding tended to polarize further. By 1916 Dorchester had six farms, only two of them owner-occupied[7] Kelly's *Directory of Oxfordshire* for 1915 shows little evidence of fresh community prosperity. Dorchester still had two inns, three pubs and two beer retailers. A motor garage, cycle agent, and Mrs Cadel's apartments at the Lilacs suggest the growing trend of visitors touring the picturesque Thames Valley and visiting the abbey and nearby archaeological sites. The cluster of Thameside villas at Burcot is

revealed by the numerous gardeners listed. Otherwise the picture is one of the standard shops and services of a large village. Religion is represented by the vicar at the vicarage, the Catholic priest, and the Missionary College. None of these would have appeared in Dorchester a century earlier, indicating the extent of the religious changes to which we now turn.

The old régime: Dorchester before 1838

The abbey in these years epitomized, in many respects, archetypal Anglican decline – in physical fabric and pastoral mission alike. As we have seen in the previous chapter, in the mid-1840s the dilapidated and cavernous church began to be restored and developed for an increasingly

48. The diminished interior before restoration, with the plaster ceiling of the 1740s cutting across the great east window. Engraved for Skelton's 'Antiquities of Oxfordshire' (1823)

different style of worship. In pastoral matters, a few years earlier, unsatisfactory structures and pressures to revive and reform had begun to lead to change in Dorchester. There was much scope for improvement.

The Clergy

The Revd James Roe was Perpetual Curate of Dorchester for 51 years, from 1787 to 1838. The living was a poor one, worth £100 per annum in 1831. Its rectorial and vicarial tithes had long been appropriated and were in lay hands, hence the relatively lowly status of the incumbent as a perpetual curate. The living remained in the gift of the Fettiplace heirs after the manorial sale of 1808. James Roe held Dorchester in plurality with the rectory of Newbury, a Crown living worth £455 per annum in 1831.[8] Predictably he chose to live in Newbury, so Dorchester was without a resident incumbent for half a century. There was a succession of curates,[9] sometimes resident, but mostly making ends meet by working in different parishes and teaching in the University or schools, although not apparently – after the mid-eighteenth century – in Dorchester's grammar school close by the abbey's west tower. Dorchester's curates included Mr Modd, chaplain of Corpus Christi College, where his 'misbehaviour, drunkenness, extravagance and other irregularities' in the 1770s and 1780s finally led to his dismissal in 1792. Nevertheless, he seems to have come out to Dorchester to serve the parishioners, on occasion during the week to help 'his deceased clerk's necessitous family'.[10] Roe paid his curates £50 per annum.

The Peculiar

Unsurprisingly Dorchester was a candidate for augmentation of the living, first from Queen Anne's Bounty and later by the Diocesan Society in Aid of Queen Anne's Bounty, set up in 1832.[11] Accountability for such funding was one element

in the modernization of Dorchester's ecclesiastical arrangements. Since the Dissolution in 1536, Dorchester had been the centre of a Peculiar Jurisdiction, holding sway over the parishes and hamlets of Benson with Roke, Burcot, Chisel hampton, Clifton Hampden, Dorchester with Overy, Drayton St Leonard, Marsh Baldon and Toot Baldon, Nettlebed with Crocker End, Pishill, Russells Water, Stadhampton, and Warborough with Shillingford. This territory echoed the area which had owed tithes to the abbey before the Dissolution, and present-day parishioners may see similarities with the area of the modern team ministry, centred on Dorchester. The Peculiar had its own registrar and court, administered by a commissary or official, who held annual visitations, usually in the abbey, before adjourning to the White Hart or George.[12] This jurisdiction took the place of both the bishop and archdeacon, increasingly to their concern, as the unsuccessful efforts of Bishop Randolph in the late eighteenth century to dissolve this independent jurisdiction show.[13]

In fact, annual visitations continued until 1834, with clergy and churchwardens of all ten parishes summoned to report on who was serving as incumbent, curate, and churchwarden; on appropriate licensing of physicians, surgeons, schoolmasters and midwives; on marriages, christenings and burials in the last church year (Lady Day to Lady Day); on the state of the church and churchyard; and on the proper completion of probate procedures (probate remaining the remit nationally of church courts until 1858). It was the Peculiar that gave permission for the re-pewing of the abbey in 1792.[14] In earlier periods failure to attend church or pay church taxes was recorded (particularly in the troubled 1660s and 1670s, when known Roman Catholics and Protestant Dissenters were officially reported). Moral charges, of fornication and producing bastard children, also appeared, the last in 1742. Some of the richest records of the Dorchester Peculiar are the wills, inventories and accounts submitted to it for grant of probate. As Leslie Wood[15] has shown, these documents offer a detailed picture of the secular world of Dorchester and south Oxfordshire in the seventeenth and eighteenth centuries – farming, crops and stock; wealth, debts and credits; crafts and trades; business links and family relationships; rooms and furniture; books and belongings. Particularly intriguing for the history of the abbey is the will of Jacob Applegarth, master of Dorchester grammar school. He had acted as scribe and executor to many Dorchester neighbours. On his own death, in 1774, he willed to his 'nephew Robert Day my gold ring which is said to be Bishop Birinus consecrated ring the first Bishop of Dorchester'. Nothing further has been found of the ring.

The efficiency and separateness of this 'peculiar' arrangement were increasingly challenged. In 1836 the Act Books of the Dorchester Peculiar end. In 1837 its last known official, the Revd George Scobbell, Curate of Nettlebed and Rector of Henley, died. After this the Peculiar came to an end. In 1838 James Roe died. The institution of the next Dorchester incumbent was the first recorded in central diocesan records. Four years before this, the Poor Law Amendment Act had ended nationally the responsibility of parishes for direct relief of local poor, in favour of large Poor Law Unions, with central workhouses regulated by detailed national government rules. The reform and rationalization of nineteenth-century Anglican-ism and of secular matters historically dealt with through parish or Peculiar was beginning to reach Dorchester.

Education
Another area of Dorchester life which, in the early nineteenth century, bore the marks of the decayed institutions of an older regime was the

grammar school, housed in the former guest house of the abbey (Fig. 32). It was established by the Fettiplaces in 1651–2 and its elaborate statutes survive.[16] However, its active life, educating boys from Dorchester and further afield, was short-lived. It had ceased to be effective by the mid-eighteenth century[17] and its registers suggest spasmodic operation even before this.[18] In 1800 a private schoolmaster took on the premises and advertised for young gentlemen pupils, including borders at twenty guineas a year, to follow a curriculum covering dancing and French.[19] Such educational private enterprise was common in Oxfordshire at this period,[20] fulfilling an obvious need for those who could afford it and where reliable schooling was not widely available. By 1833 the Dorchester school had fifty pupils,[21] but this did not mean that the children of Dorchester in general had access to free or affordable elementary education. Despite the three paying day schools recorded in 1815, it was reported in 1818 that the poor of Dorchester were 'completely destitute' of education.[22]

Religion and educational provision were inextricably connected in nineteenth-century communities, but Dorchester was late to embark on this. The first Sunday school was begun in 1819. A free, National school, under the aegis of the National Society for Promoting the Education of the Poor in the Principles of the Established Church, was set up for girls and infants in 1836 on land given by the Earl of Abingdon (now the site of the Village Hall).[23] In 1858 the old grammar school was converted as an additional, National school for boys.[24] New and extended school buildings, and energetic teaching and catechizing within them, did eventually become a major focus of Anglican activity in Dorchester. Until the mid-1830s there was little evidence of action. This relative torpor was to be increasingly overtaken by changes which heralded a new and different phase of religious life in Dorchester.

Revival and competition: religion in Dorchester c.1835–1856

Vigorous and varied religious activity, rivalry and controversy were the order of the day by the mid-nineteenth century. A new Baptist chapel was built in Watling Lane, opening in 1837. At Bridge End a Primitive Methodist chapel and schoolroom were built by local labourers and opened in 1839. In 1848 the newly built St Birinus's Roman Catholic church was consecrated and the adjoining Georgian house at Bridge End given by the Davey family as a presbytery. As for the Anglicans, Roe was succeeded by resident clergy, albeit by three different incumbents in twelve years, and without an adequate parsonage.[25] The National School was now operating. Perhaps most striking of all was the first great phase of restoration and rebuilding of the abbey (1844-52) to the designs of Butterfield. As we have seen, the setting for worship was transformed, low (mainly free) pews allowing the eye to focus on the slightly raised altar, backed by a brightly coloured, polychromatic, tiled reredos.

Butterfield's work was controversial, both with contemporaries and later observers. His raising of the chancel roof and addition (or was it restoration?) of the rose tracery at the apex of the east window was still, in 1906, causing Henry Taunt to comment that 'the rose in some lights gives the idea of a horrible grinning face of a satyr, and altogether seems an error on the part of the architect'.[26] Contemporary controversy extended to the new seating arrangements, which moved one of the churchwardens, Henry J. Hannam of Burcot, to publish a pamphlet[27] strongly arguing (in a view typical of Tractarians*) that access to all seats in church should be

free, according to 'the express Word of God'. The Church of England suffered greatly from the exclusion of the poor and nothing should be done which might deter the working classes from worship. Hannam also argued for the restoration of 'the still partially existing practice in the congregation' of men sitting on the north and women separately on the south side of the central aisle.

A snapshot of how local people were responding to all this religious provision is offered by the local returns to the first and only national census of religious provision and attendance, taken in March 1851.

The religious census returns are known by historians to require careful interpretation.[28] For example, totals of worshippers for each Sunday service may include some attending more than one service. Moreover the census was controversial, especially with Anglicans (amongst whom Bishop Wilberforce of Oxford was a leading national spokesman), who considered the exercise intrusive and flawed. Their criticism was renewed when the national results of the census were known. These revealed first, that Dissenters provided nearly half of church accommodation, nearly 40% of those worshipping in the morning and afternoon, and two-thirds of evening worshippers; and secondly, that an estimated 42% of potential worshippers stayed away from church and chapel altogether. These findings added to the sense of threat to the Church of England's status as the national church felt by Anglicans at the time. They also reinforced fears that people were being lost to

---

★ Tractarianism was a name given to the earlier stages of the Oxford Movement. The name was taken from the *Tracts for the Times* (1833-41), in which the founders of this High Church Anglican movement (including Newman, Pusey and Keble) developed its beliefs and aims. Tractarianism and related ritualism were to become major influences on the abbey and local community in Dorchester.

organized religion on a large scale, particularly from the working classes. One reaction was to claim that non-Anglicans had exaggerated their numbers, as did the Revd William Addison, incumbent of Dorchester from 1850 to 1856, who told Bishop Wilberforce in 1854 that he had been 'strongly impressed with the palpable exaggeration on the part of the Romanists and Baptists'.[29] Others, perhaps like churchwarden Hannam, pressed for greater efforts to attract worshippers from all classes.

Dorchester's religious census returns are more complicated than most (Table 1). Addison made no return. He was probably part of the 27% of Oxfordshire parsons (as against a national figure of 10% non-respondent Anglican clergy) who refused to complete some or all of the census. A proxy is provided by the generalized figures for attendance at the abbey supplied by Addison at the Bishop's Visitation of 1854, and by the more detailed responses of his successor, the Revd William Macfarlane, in 1857. The Roman Catholic return has a wrong date for their church, whilst the Baptists record 26 sittings, all free, yet claim attendances of 76 and 100. Amidst all this complication and controversy, what can be said about how far Dorchester's population of 1,061 were religiously observant, and about how the competitive battles between denominations were going? On the basis of an Anglican attendance of 300 (using Macfarlane's count) and adding all other attendances, 676 (64% of the population) worshipped on census Sunday. This may have included some Catholics and Baptists

DENOMINATION	DATE BUILDING ERECTED	NUMBER OF SITTINGS	ATTENDANCES			RETURN MADE BY
			Morning	Afternoon	Evening	
Church of England	Before 1800	800[1]	400[2] 250 (plus children)[3]			(No return made. Information from other sources)
Roman Catholic	1828–9[4]	65 (50 free)	60	60		Robert Newsham, priest, Dorchester
Baptist	About 1837	26 (all free)		76	100	John Oldham, minister, Wallingford
Primitive Methodist	1839	150 (132 free)			80	G. Wallis, minister, Wallingford

Notes
1. 1866 Bishop's Visitation Returns (OA MS. Oxf. Dioc. c 332, f. 17). The 1914 return gives 'church accommodation' as 578, ibid., c 377, f. 283.
2. E. P. Baker (ed.), Bishop Wilberforce's Visitation Returns for the Archdeaconry of Oxford 1854,

Oxfordshire Record Society, vol. 35 (1954), pp. 49–50.
3. 1857 Bishop's Visitation Returns (OA MS. Oxf. Dioc. d 179).
4. Seemingly an error, as all other references give 1848 as the date of building.

Table 1. Church and chapel in Dorchester: 1851 religious census returns (total population 1,061)

going to more than one service, arguably a significant measure of support in itself. Some historians, seeking to allow for possible double counting, have used only the figures for the best-attended service. On this basis Dorchester had 540 worshippers, 51% of its population. So there were absentees. Of those attending, the abbey had the largest congregations, but other denominations were appealing in contrasting ways to sizeable numbers of local people. Other sources take us beyond the headcounts of worshippers in 1851.

The Roman Catholics

Dorchester's Roman Catholic congregation, their recent church and their resident priest represented a new flowering of a long local presence. Dorchester, Overy, Burcot and Clifton Hampden had been a significant focus of the old faith since the late sixteenth century. The core of support came from some of Dorchester's longest-standing families – the Daveys, the Princes and the Days. This gave local Catholicism a distinctive character. Unlike other Oxfordshire centres, the faith was not dependent on a leading landed family and the protection of a 'big house'. Rather, an interrelated group of yeoman and tenant families, important and accepted figures in the local community, sustained support, leading the historian of post-Reformation Catholicism in Oxfordshire to describe Dorchester as a 'nursing home of the Old Faith during the dark years between the accession of the Stuarts and the nineteenth century'.[30]

In the anxious and uncertain days after the Restoration the minister of Dorchester, the Revd David Thomas, wrote in 1662 to his ecclesiastical superiors, 'There is one of o[u]r neighbours dead at Dorchester John Day ye elder a Catholicke his sones desire that he might have Christian buriall which I dare not grant

him without your allowance.' The next day the ecclesiastical official decreed, 'I know nothing but that a Catholick may have Christian buriall,' and John Day's funeral is indeed recorded in Dorchester's parish registers.[31] Forty-nine Days were buried at Dorchester Abbey between 1639 and 1836; forty-six Daveys between 1642 and 1831; and thirty-four Princes between 1662 and 1828. Tombstones in the abbey churchyard bear witness to the continuity and status of these families, and to the pragmatic co-existence operating in Dorchester between Anglicans and Catholics (Fig. 52).

Notwithstanding this, Catholics operated under varying degrees of disadvantage right into the nineteenth century. They were granted freedom of worship and schooling only in 1791. Catholic Emancipation – the lifting of legal, fiscal and political disabilities – came in 1829. During the eighteenth century local Catholics survived in small numbers – thirteen recorded in Dorchester, Burcot and Clifton in 1676; twelve in 1706; ten in 1769; and eighteen in 1780.[32] By the mid-eighteenth century Catholicism was sustained chiefly by missioner priests and/or domestic family chapels, which co-religionists might also attend. Missioner priests are recorded at Dorchester in the 1750s and in 1773.[33] Between 1765 and 1787 the chapel of the Simeon, later the Weld, family at Britwell House some miles to the east became the focus. In 1793 St Ignatius' Catholic church was established in St Clements, Oxford, and close ties developed between it and the Catholic community in Dorchester.[34]

Throughout all of this, the Daveys maintained a domestic chapel at Overy, a small cluster of houses and cottages ending at Overy Mill and tucked away off the main road. 'The old chapel house was at the end of a by-lane and being enclosed by rickyards, gardens and orchards, did not in any way challenge the

49. Overy, a secluded hamlet of Dorchester, was home to both recusant Catholics and early Protestant dissenters in the 17th century (© Oxfordshire County Council Photographic Archive)

curiosity or suspicion of poursuivants.'[35] It was also at Overy, in the period of prosecution of non-Anglicans after 1660, that Protestant Dissenters found a place to worship, being reported to the Official of Dorchester Peculiar in 1673 as a 'Phanatick brood' in 'the Barne at Overy'.[36] As to the Daveys' chapel, a missioner priest recorded in the 1770s that it had 'all necessary Altar-Furniture' and was regularly used, 'some week day during each Indulgence or thereabouts'.[37] (The building was finally demolished in 1877.) From 1796 to 1802 Overy was served by French priests from Thame.[38] It was during this time that the Daveys gave shelter to an eminent refugee from the French Revolution, Michael Desvalpons, Archdeacon and

Vicar-General of Dol, Brittany, who was buried and memorialized in the south aisle of the abbey, at the behest of the Warden of New College, Oxford.

In the early nineteenth century local Catholics were served by a priest from St Clements, in Oxford, on alternate Sundays. From 1823 this role was undertaken by Father Robert Newsham, subsequently the first priest of the new church of St Birinus,[39] consecrated in August 1849 by Bishop Ullathorne, who, on the restoration of a Catholic hierarchy to England in 1850, became the first Catholic Bishop of Birmingham. The new church was paid for by John Davey (1787–1864) and designed in Gothic Decorated style by William

50. St Birinus Roman Catholic church opened in 1848 as the first public place of Catholic worship in Dorchester since the Reformation. It was paid for by the Davey family, in whose house at Overy the old faith had been observed in a private chapel.

Wilkinson Wardell, a pupil of Pugin. Wardell went on to design Catholic cathedrals in Sydney and Melbourne, but at Dorchester he worked on a small, finely detailed scale. The decorative scheme and dedication to Birinus identified the church with Dorchester's importance from earliest Christianization. Glass, rood screen, statuary and paintings were given by various members of the Davey family and by Father Newsham. Items and vestments from the chapel at Overy were transferred to the new church. Newsham is also said to have brought to Bridge House, beside the church, the school for boys he had previously run at St Clements.[40] Thus Dorchester Catholicism in the mid-nineteenth century combined old and new elements. The continuity was provided particularly by the Daveys, by links back to Birinus, and in the continued gathering of worshippers from a wider area to one of the still relatively few places of Catholic worship. More novel were the confidence and opportunity to develop a public and independent face in the changed legal and theological climate of the more pluralist 1840s and 1850s.

The Primitive Methodists

There was little traditional, by contrast, about the Primitive Methodists. Their church had broken away from the increasingly conservative Wesleyan Methodists in 1811. It offered a direct and personal religious experience through initial conversion and salvation and then in active worship and membership led by local lay preachers. The Ranters, as hostile contemporaries labelled them, had a reputation for zealous enthusiasm and radicalism. When seven local labourers bought a plot 36 feet by 22 feet (11 by 6.7 m) at Bridge End for £5 in 1839[41] and began to build by their own labour, before and after work, a mud-walled chapel and school, the way had not been easy. John Petty's *History of the Primitive Methodist Connexion* (1864) recounts that at Dorchester

the missionaries had to encounter the most formidable and determined opposition, and to endure violent and brutal persecution. For some time they were stoned both as they entered and left the village on Sabbath mornings. On one occasion Mrs Wheeldon was hit on the eye with a stone . . . and another member of society had two of his teeth knocked out with a stone. A number of young persons of the baser sort were encouraged in their savage treatment of preachers by some in the higher classes. . . . A pious and humane gentleman wished to persuade them to discontinue their visits, saying the ruffians would no more mind killing one of them than killing a dog. But the heroic missionaries were not to be easily persuaded to do this. . . . And deliverance came at length. Several of the gentlemen who had been the abettors in the persecution were suddenly arrested by affliction, and in a few days were called into the presence of their Maker. This event produced a deep and solemn impression among the inhabitants, and the persecutors soon afterwards ceased to stone the preachers. When the dreadful storm of persecution was passed over the good seed which had been sown sprang up, and the society flourished. Several of the persecutors were subdued by the power of divine grace, and were made new creatures in Christ Jesus among others the constable, who had frequently been employed by the gentlemen to drive the preachers from the village, and who had been a great drunkard, was converted to the Lord and became a new man. A cottage was obtained for preaching during the winter, and this becoming too small, efforts were made to secure a new

chapel. A site was obtained for the purpose, many of the former opponents rendered cheerful assistance, and the humble sanctuary was opened for worship on the 18th September 1839.

Although the tale has lost nothing in the telling by the movement's historian, the strength of reaction to this new kind of religion in Dorchester's midst is clear. Nevertheless, the Primitive Methodists persisted with, as we have seen, eighty reported worshippers in 1851. In March that year the original conveyance and trust of 1839 was extended.[42] Just one of the founders, William Brown, remained and six new names were added. The distinctive and independent form of worship was finding a response in Dorchester, just one of the choices people were making in their religion. Indeed, when the parson was asked in 1854 by his bishop to state the number of Dissenters he could not, 'as many persons go occasionally to church and to the meeting house and parents of families in some cases are dissenters'.[43] This last remark presumably reflected the fact that the only available day schools were Anglican.

The struggles in Dorchester were not only between denominations but also with alternative cultures, indifferent to organized religion. The churchwardens' accounts (1837–43) include payments to the parish constable to visit pubs on Sundays at the time of divine service. In 1847 the ladies of Dorchester complained of nuisances committed on the seats on the bridge, which were said to be a disgrace to the parish. The remedy was 'to slope them up with brickwork . . . so that no person can stand or sit on them'.[44] (The marks of the infilling can still be seen today.) In 1857 the vicar reflected that, despite the abbey, two dissenting chapels and 'a Romanist chapel', 'many of the adults are careless and go to no place of worship. . . . The people are generally

	1852	1863	1873	1883	1891	1907	1915	1939
Church of England	X	X	X	X	X	X	X	X
Baptist		X	X					
Primitive Methodist		X	X					
Roman Catholic		X	X	X	X	X	X	X
Wesleyan Methodist						X		
Presbyterian	X							

Table 2. Church and chapel in Dorchester: 1852–1939 (Source: Commercial directories for Oxfordshire)

well affected but the adult population for the most part very ignorant . . . few of the grown up men come to church.'[45]

Nevertheless, the mid-century was to prove a peak of religious activity in Dorchester, as Table 2 shows.

Anglican assertion and Tractarian triumph: 1856–1885

The appointment, in 1856, of a new incumbent, the Revd William Charles Macfarlane, was to prove a watershed in the religious life of Dorchester. This 'devoted and generous minister with a private fortune'[46] became perpetual curate two years after his ordination in 1854 by Bishop Wilberforce of Oxford and four years after graduating from Magdalen College, Oxford. He stayed until his death in 1885. The continuity and style of Macfarlane's ministry reflected not only his individual qualities but, for Dorchester, a final leaving behind of the anachronistic vestiges of earlier ecclesiastical arrangements. Macfarlane's energetic and resident pastorate matched the broader expectations of clergy now current in

the diocese of the reforming Samuel Wilberforce (Bishop of Oxford, 1845–69) and in the Church of England at large. It was also to be a striking example of the implementation of a High Church, Tractarian ideal,[47] seeking to re-create the parish as an all-encompassing focus of Christian fellowship and spiritual and practical provision in a changing world, a dynamic entity which would meet the needs, and command the allegiance, of all. Macfarlane, with his Oxford background and the independence brought by private income, had the conviction and the means to put this ideal into action.

Macfarlane began on a necessarily practical note. He built a vicarage. This substantial house (Fig. 42), designed by David Brandon in the 'Parsonage Gothic' style and close to the abbey, was an essential prerequisite of the 'new ministry', signalling residence, appropriate status and domesticity. (Rather than the married family ideal, the bachelor Macfarlane's household consisted in 1871 of his unmarried sister and housekeeper, three nieces – all clergymen's daughters – two house servants, a cook and a groom.)[48] Macfarlane became resident in Dorchester in April 1857.[49]

Until *c.*1870 much of Macfarlane's effort, and money, was channelled into the abbey building, which remained dilapidated and dangerous in parts. Butterfield's earlier restoration had been confined to the sanctuary, chancel and east end of the nave. Work was renewed under the eminent and less contentious architect George Gilbert Scott, culminating, in 1873–4, in restoration of the south-east aisle roof and chapel, a new organ, and new marble steps and reredos to the high altar. This was a fitting finale. The altar of the south-east chapel was dedicated to Bishop Wilberforce (died 1873), who had done so much to reform and revive Anglicanism in Oxfordshire and to protect High Church clergy, whilst the elaborations of the sanctuary and high altar provided a setting for the liturgical changes which Macfarlane had been introducing with increasing confidence.

The availability of daily services and frequent celebrations of Holy Communion were primary tenets of Tractarianism. These should be offered by clergy and choir, suitably robed, impressing and inspiring a congregation much less directly involved in worship than in the previous auditory style. Macfarlane found that he had a long way to go to achieve this ideal. In 1857 Holy Communion was celebrated only once a month and at great festivals, with forty to fifty communicants. There were two Sunday services, two sermons a week, and morning prayer on two weekdays and saints' days.[50] Macfarlane developed a choir, said on occasions to number over 100.[51] In 1861 psalms began to be chanted by the choir, rather than sung by the congregation.[52] By 1866, Holy Communion was being celebrated every Sunday, and twice on the first Sunday of the month and great festivals. There were two Sunday sermons, daily services and 100 communicants at great festivals, although still forty on average.[53] By 1875 the full measure of change was apparent. Macfarlane, now assisted by a curate,

offered the Sacrament at daily services, on the first Sunday and great festivals at 7, 9 and 11.45 am and every other Sunday at 8 and 11.45 am. In all there were about 450 celebrations of Holy Communion each year. Matins and Evensong took place daily at 7.30 am and 7 pm, times intended to be convenient to working people. The number and timing of Sunday communion services was especially significant, as Macfarlane indicated to the bishop:

> of the communicants; ¾ always communicate early – thus signifying their acceptance of the highest form of ritual: while those who prefer the plain service, have it monthly and on great festivals at 11.45.

The number of communicants on great festivals had risen to 180.[54] Macfarlane trod carefully and gradually, but determinedly, towards his ideal pattern of worship and liturgy in the setting of a fully restored and beautified abbey. Dorchester became well known for its ritual. Macfarlane was admitted in 1870 to the Society of the Holy Cross, the earliest (established in 1855) and most select (its members were all clergy) of the ritualist societies.[55] When, in 1874, *The Tourist's Church Guide* was published,[56] listing all churches in England and Wales using those marks of ritualism, lighted candles and eucharistic vestments, Dorchester was included. Its daily communion and use of Gregorian chant were noted. Macfarlane was later said to have made Dorchester the local headquarters of the High Church.[57]

Dorchester's transformation was a striking example of the diffusion within the Church of England of Oxford Movement ideas and practices. Beginning in 1833, it has been estimated that by 1840 there were 91 Tractarian parish priests and, by 1870, 442 (about a quarter of them ritualists),[58] so Macfarlane was one of a growing band. This expansion was a particular feature of the ten years before 1874, a date signif- icant for the passing of the Public Worship Regulation Act, a largely ineffective attempt to legislate for the prosecution and imprisonment of Anglican clergy allegedly conducting worship outside defined Protestant rubrics. The Act's pas- sage was a measure of the acute sensitivities and bitter controversies raised by ritualist parochial practice. Dorchester, in one of the five dioceses with the highest concentrations of High Church- men and ritualists,[59] was part of this. Hence Macfarlane's careful explanation of 1875 to his bishop of the two kinds of communion service he offered, in order to meet the differing wishes of parishioners.

Once the restoration of the abbey was largely complete, Macfarlane turned his efforts, and his funds, to other projects in the parish. This di- versification included the building of a dual- purpose school-church at Burcot in 1869 and of a new girls' and infants' school in Dorchester in

1872 and the foundation of a missionary college, housed in converted and extended buildings bought by Macfarlane adjoining the High Street (Fig. 45). The College opened in 1878 to train young men for Anglican ordination and mission- ary work abroad. Resident student numbers built up to twenty and then to twenty-four; by 1914 a total of 192 had been trained, 94% of whom worked overseas. The college had a very definite impact on Dorchester, perhaps approaching Butterfield's High Church hope for a college of priests forging the ideal local Christian commu- nity. The clerical presence seen around the vil- lage grew. The principal and vice-principal of the college contributed to abbey services. College students were 'the backbone of the Abbey choir'; gave concerts for the locals; played them at cricket and football, and swam and rowed; and helped run the vicar's boys' club. The chairman of the newly created parish council for its first five years from 1894 was the principal

51. The new National School for girls and infants of 1871–2, designed by G. G. Scott (© Oxfordshire County Council Photographic Archive)

of the Missionary College.[60] The college's ultimate purpose was ministry elsewhere but its presence in Dorchester added to the growing and high profile work of Anglicanism under Macfarlane. He and his curate were constantly in the schools during the week, busy with Sunday schools, night school, Bible classes, two services a week at Burcot, a guild for those wishing to keep their baptismal vows, and so on.

Alongside all of this, the active dissenting presence seems to have diminished (Table 2). Macfarlane claimed, in 1866,[61] that 'dissent is very much on the decrease', whilst Roman Catholicism was confined to one family (presumably the Daveys) and their dependants. Perhaps the zeal and resources of the re-energized Church of England were too much for the Baptists and Primitive Methodists to contend with. Certainly they fade from the records after the late 1870s, a time when Dorchester's declining economy was eroding the already slender resources of these small chapels. As for the Roman Catholics, they were faced by High Church Anglican assertions that it was the Church of England that represented the true English Catholic church. This, and the contemporary climate of anti-ritualism and fear of conversion to Rome, did not make for easy tolerance. The difficulties of coexistence emerged in a burial case which made Dorchester briefly nationally notorious.

John Davey, founder and benefactor of St Birinus's Catholic Church, died in November 1863. He was buried in the abbey churchyard by the Anglican vicar, Macfarlane. William S. Blackstone, former MP for Wallingford and an anti-ritualist,[62] saw the burial and wrote about it to John Walter, proprietor of *The Times*. Seventeen years later, in 1880, when the Commons was debating a Burials Bill to provide for burial of the dead by their own ministers – following notorious instances of Church of England

52. Amongst the Catholic gravestones in the abbey churchyard is this one to John Davey (d.1863), benefactor of the new Catholic church, whose funeral became part of national controversies over the burial rights of non-Anglicans

clergy refusing to bury non-Anglicans in churchyards, which were the only local burial places – John Walter, by now MP for Berkshire, cited Davey's burial at Dorchester in support of the legislation:

I remember . . . the funeral of a much respected Roman Catholic at Dorchester, in Oxfordshire, whose ancestors were in the churchyard for many generations. The Roman

75

Catholic Bishop attended at the grave, when, in order to show their distaste to a Protestant service, he and all the relatives turned round their backs to the officiating clergyman. I never have forgotten the scene, and in order to prevent such a repetition I gladly accept the measure which will allow their burial by their own pastors.[63]

A furore followed. The Davey nephews denied any disrespect. Dr Ullathorne, the Roman Catholic Bishop of Birmingham, confirmed that he had celebrated a Requiem Mass at St Birinus's Church but had not attended the graveside service, and Macfarlane wrote publically to the Daveys refuting Blackstone's charges and recollecting that 'several [family] members attended who behaved with great decorum during the service'.

The controversy was laid to rest, but it revealed the difficult, sometimes volatile nature of this period of Dorchester's religious history. Out of it came, by the time of Macfarlane's death in 1885, Anglican domination and increasing diversification into a great array of educational, welfare, social and leisure activities. Above all, there was daily, often choral, worship in the newly restored abbey, centred on a dramatic altar,[64] now raised and framed by its carved reredos and paintings.

1886-1920: certainties challenged?

'Doubt, which is destructive in most things, is especially so in matters of Religion.'[65] These words of the Revd Nathaniel Poyntz, Vicar of Dorchester from 1886 to 1920, sum up much of his approach. He shared Macfarlane's High Churchmanship and sought to maintain his ideal of a Tractarian parish. Since graduating from Pembroke College, Oxford, in 1868, Poyntz had served a number of curacies, including that of

53. Revd Nathaniel Poyntz, vicar from 1886 to 1920

St Mathias, Stoke Newington, well known for its ritualism.[66] Unlike Macfarlane, Poyntz demonstrated no tolerance or gradualism in his approach at Dorchester. His stance on doctrine and liturgy was uncompromising. His attitude leaps off the pages of the *Dorchester Parish Magazine*, instituted by him and used to meet doctrinal controversies head-on and to find every aspect of local life relevant to his role as spiritual director and natural community leader. Thus he wrote not only of the true meaning of the Sacrament but on everything from the quality of football and cricket teams to parliamentary elections.

For example, Poyntz began 1901 with a series of articles on the true nature of the Book of Common Prayer, arguing close coincidence and continuity between it and the pre-Reformation

Missal. He was always dismissive of the claimed significance of what he unfailingly referred to as 'the so-called Reformation' and concluded that the Anglican Church always intended 'to preserve the same faith about the Sacrament that it had held before the reign of Henry VIII'.

The Anglican Church intends its priests at the Altar to cause the Bread and Wine to become really the Body and Blood of Christ on the Altar, and that he should really give the Body and Blood of Christ to the Communicants.

PRICE ONE PENNY.

THE

PARISH MAGAZINE

✠ DORCHESTER, OXON. ✠

NO. 181.

JANUARY, 1901.

— PUBLISHED MONTHLY. —

Communications to be addressed to The VICAR.

Printed by W. D. Jenkins, "Advertiser" Office, Wallingford.

54. The Dorchester Parish Magazine. Founded by Poyntz, its pages reflect his emphatically High Church doctrine and his all-encompassing involvement in local life. (© Oxfordshire County Council Photographic Archive)

What a shocking thing it would be for the Priests to give the Sacrament to Communicants saying it was the Body of Jesus Christ and the Blood of Jesus Christ, if after all it is only in itself Bread and Wine! What a deception! And, we would even say, what a blasphemous deception!

In July he discussed the use of vestments and processions, writing enthusiastically about a visit to Brittany and the Corpus Christi celebrations he had seen there. The use of incense and the raising of the altar ('lifting up the sacrifice') were energetically defended. To Poyntz the conclusion was obvious: 'We must not be surprised therefore if after all we find our religion is very much like the Roman Catholic religion, or ought to be so if the Prayer Book is used rightly.'

Sustaining the forms of worship which the Vicar considered so vital was demanding.[67] Poyntz expressed frustration at the weak and fitful singing of the all-male choir, disappointed in 1901 that only 'ordinary simple music' was possible. Shortly afterwards, ritualism again attracted parliamentary attention through the Royal Commission on Ecclesiastical Discipline, evidence to which listed churches in 1903 with more extreme forms of ritual, for example, the use of incense. Such practices have been associated particularly with larger urban communities but Dorchester is cited in the Royal Commission report as an example of High Church ritualism in country parishes.[68] Evidence was given by two locally resident witnesses,[69] both members of the Church Association, established in 1865 to counteract ritualism in the Church of England. In all, the Association submitted critical accounts of services at ninety-one churches in various parts of England. James Denman attended Dorchester Abbey in May 1904 and saw vestments, incense, lighted candles, wafers not bread at Communion, mixing of wine and water in the chalice, the

55. Classroom in Dorchester girls' school on 4 April 1905. The style of the Church teaching here was reported to the Bishop of Oxford and to the Royal Commission on Ecclesiastical Discipline (1905). (© Oxfordshire County Council Photographic Archive)

elevation of the sacred elements, and genuflection at the consecration, followed by the priest (whose earlier actions were obscured) turning to the congregation saying 'Behold the lamb of God.' The catalogue of ritualist offences at Dorchester also included calling the service the Mass, crucifixes and the stations of the cross in church, and crucifixes and sacred heart images of Mary and Christ in the girls National school, where pupils were taught to say 'Hail Marys'. Denman claimed that 'nearly half the parishioners' were deterred from attending church by these illegal and Romish practices.

George Randell Higgins (of The Croft, Burcot) described a mission room opened in the village in 1902 to provide a 'Church of England' service, and claimed it was oversubscribed by disaffected parishioners. Services at the Roman Catholic church were 'less extreme' than those at the abbey, whilst the parish magazine was unfit for circulation because of 'extreme Romish

teaching'. At Burcot the school managers had directed removal of the stations of the cross from the dual-purpose school-church, but the vicar replaced them every Sunday.

Poyntz, given opportunity to respond, felt he had been targeted by the Church Association and claimed that most of the practices had applied for 'over thirty years', that is from Macfarlane's time. However, he had ceased to declare 'Behold the lamb of God', or to instruct the school girls to say 'Hail Marys', 'in deference to the wish of the Bishop of Oxford'. The comments of Bishop Paget of Oxford, seen as sympathetic to the High Church view, are revealing.[70] Sixteen churches in his diocese were cited. As a Commissioner himself, Paget sought to be neutral. His position should be 'to encourage and help on the good work of High-Churchmen and Low-Churchmen alike . . . [it is] a better use of my life than if I spent it struggling . . . to bring the diocese to any precision of uniformity.' He was drawn on only two cases, Headington and Dorchester. At Dorchester 'the use made of the schools . . . has given great offence. . . . Both recently and at an earlier date [I] requested the vicar to abandon practices which seemed to me both serious and plainly indefensible; . . . he has complied. Nevertheless, I should not feel that I had written frankly if I refrained from saying that I can well understand the feeling that was evinced in the evidence to the Commission.' This is an oblique but emphatic singling out of Poyntz's troublesome and harmful behaviour, especially in the Dorchester schools. This must have been damaging, not only within the local community but also more widely to the Church of England, as it argued for continued state funding of denominational schools in the period of the controversial 1902 Education Act.

The Bishop of Oxford at his next visitation in 1906 included additional questions, betraying the sensitivity of the times. At Dorchester, Poyntz replied with care. Yes, incense was used at the consecration 'but not ceremonially'; the sacrament was not reserved; no images with lights or flowers were kept; 'the whole or main part of the Canon of the Mass, according to the Roman or Sarum use' was kept on the Altar 'for private devotion'. Asked if any hymns, prayers or devotions involving Invocation of or Devotion to the Blessed Virgin Mary or the Saints were used, his answer was particularly pointed – yes, the Book of Common Prayer.[71]

Outside the abbey church, Poyntz's energies and certainties were reflected in a wealth of other activities: the schools, Sunday school, Maternity Society, cricket and football clubs,

56. *Boys of the abbey choir and a priest (probably from the Missionary College), c.1900 (© Oxfordshire County Council Photographic Archive)*

Friendly Societies, Crysanthemum Society, Missionary Work Party, Confraternity of the Blessed Sacrament, night school, boys' club, Horticultural Society, rummage sales, amateur theatricals – these were some of the organizations in which the vicar or his wife took a leading role. Committees, minutes and votes of thanks, the vicar taking the chair, were the order of the day.

The young were particularly targeted, using a carrot and stick approach. The clergy were in the schools five days a week. In 1896–7 a new school for boys, replacing the old grammar school building, opened, and in 1900 the girls' and infants' school was enlarged. A Sunday afternoon children's service was introduced. There was much emphasis on prizes, properly earned. Non-attendance at Sunday school would, as the vicar regularly pointed out in the magazine, mean no gift at the annual treat and losing points for the Clothing Club. There were also reminders that children should not be led to think that they could get on in life 'just as well as other people, though they are lazy and do not exert themselves. There is a false kindness and we must not encourage it. True mercy and kindness is that of God, who will reward every man according to his work.'[72] Girls not in school for prayers before the start of lessons were told that they could not expect God's blessing to be equally upon them. There are hints that the school regime was not always tranquilly accepted; in March 1901 the vicar had cause to upbraid angry mothers for allowing 'themselves to get tempestuous over things' and going to the school to confront teachers about treatment of their children. He pointed out that children went 'to learn something, and to be educated in good manners' so rules were necessary. All complaints must be directed to him.

There was no question of giving up on older parishioners. Men's and boys' clubs were run in

the winter months, although in 1899 they were closed because of bad behaviour. Trying again in 1901, Poyntz warned that noise or bad behaviour would lead to the expulsion of the culprits. For adults as for children, gifts were strictly conditional. For example, the Maternity Society offered help only after the birth of a third child and provided it was 'in wedlock, there being no sinful slur on the birth of the first'. Neither would any help be offered to those married in a register office, 'as the blessing of God has not been given to such unions'.[73] These attempts to be *the* providers of education and welfare in Dorchester were matched by efforts to offer suitable and rational leisure pursuits, of which there was a formidable calendar throughout the year, incorporating both religious festivals and traditional events like May Day and Harvest Home.

The degree to which the Church could reach into the lives of Dorchester people during this period is well conveyed by the case of Frederick Hawes, who died of meningitis aged 23 in September 1901.[74] He attended the local church school, joined the abbey choir aged 7, was confirmed and become a communicant. He was a bell-ringer, took part in village plays and was described by Poyntz as an exemplary son and brother and an industrious and painstaking workman. His chief recreation was painting. He was buried in cassock and surplice, his coffin borne by old school friends and bell-ringers, and he was accompanied by the vicar (who had relaxed his usual prohibition on Sunday funerals for the convenience of the family), the clergy and students of the missionary college, the abbey choir and many members of his family and friends. A muffled peal was rung on the abbey bells. Here, it seems, was Poyntz's ideal parishioner. How many were there like him?

Nathaniel Poyntz's incumbency at Dorchester coincided with a period seen as one of crisis by

*57 (above) and 58.
By the late 19th century,
the Church of England
was providing not only
worship and schooling in
Dorchester but also a
whole range of organiza-
tions, events and festivals,
as here on May Day in
the vicarage garden and at
a village festival (Poyntz
stands to the left of the
carriage). Both c.1900.
(© Oxfordshire County
Council Photographic
Archive)*

contemporaries and later historians, both for the Church of England and for religion generally. Forces of secularization, as well as internal stresses in Anglicanism, had it seems become irrefutable. Does the experience of Dorchester show these processes at work? Secularization may be defined in various ways; as a loss of faith, perhaps in the face of new sources of explanation, or (and this is easier for historians to measure) as a decline in participation in organized religion. *The Dorchester Parish Magazine* and other sources do reveal the latter, showing that, for all its undoubted dominance of formal religion in Dorchester by this time, Anglicanism was in a static or declining state. Numbers of communicants at Christmas, Easter and Whitsuntide, the maximum times of attendance, were 50 in 1857; 100 in 1866; 180 in 1875; 166 in 1887; and 124 in 1901.[75] The growth of the 1860s and 1870s had found its limits. Support was declining.

The growth had not transferred itself to other churches. Dorchester's other Protestant denomi-nations had almost disappeared. In 1881 the Primitive Methodist chapel had been sold back to the Cherrills for £20. By then its trustees were a wheelwright from Crowmarsh Gifford and a bootmaker from Long Wittenham. In 1888 the property was sold again, to no less than William Booth of the Salvation Army, on a mortgage of £50. No records have emerged of a functioning Salvation Army Citadel in Dorchester and, by 1897, Booth was seeking to sell, willing to accept £12 10s. The prospective purchaser was none other than Poyntz, in line with his policy of seeking to buy out rivals. (In this case the property title was insufficiently clear to proceed.[76]) Poyntz did, however, buy the 'cottage chapel and garden' of the Baptists for £16 in 1908 from five trustees, none of them local. The property acquired a restrictive covenant forbidding any use for religious services 'by Non-conformists of any sect or denomination'.[77] The Roman Catholics continued, with the patron, Robert Davey, striving to stir the local priest and prolific novelist, William Barry (1885–1907), into

59. A funeral procession at Dorchester c. 1910, with robed clergy and choir, very like that of Frederick Hawes, described here (© Oxfordshire County Council Photographic Archive)

greater parochial action.[78] However, a negative milestone was reached when, in 1901, the last Davey resident at Overy died.

The end of an era?

Looking back from Poyntz's death in 1920, the transformations to both the abbey and the wider religious life of Dorchester since the days of James Roe were undoubtedly vast.

The experience of religious revival and vigour in the second quarter of the nineteenth century was shared across denominations. Dorchester had never been a single church place. As it went through a period of sometimes difficult change and also one when Catholics and Protestant Dissenters were achieving new legal recognition, religious pluralism became a reality as never before or since. However, as the 1851 religious census showed, Dorchester was some way from a totally observant society, even at this relatively high watermark.

The historically dominant Church of England finally threw off pastoral inadequacies and anomalous constraints, including its Peculiar status. It took on changed roles, lessened in some respects such as poor relief, and increased in others such as education. The living remained a poor one, whilst the expectations of what the clergy should offer rose greatly. The new parochial ideal came nearest to realization after 1856, when Dorchester had an incumbent, Macfarlane, who combined resident and highly motivated pastoral care, patient gradualism, and private means, all at a time of relative prosperity in the parish and when other denominations had become relatively weak.

In the second half of the century, a vital change came when Anglicanism in Dorchester took on the intensely parochial focus of Tractarianism, delivered first in the abbey and its liturgy and then across the whole spectrum of 'non-religious' welfare, educational and social functions. Pluralism faded, as (from the mid-1870s) did Dorchester's economic fortunes and population size.

The success of Tractarian Anglicanism was not sustained after Macfarlane's death in 1885. There was inevitably less emphasis on major new achievements, such as restoration of the abbey, new schools, or the missionary college, and more on sustaining this dauntingly far-reaching operation. Dorchester was becoming less prosperous, and clergy incomes were falling (Poyntz claimed in 1899 that, after outgoings, only £1 14s 1½d of his combined income of £209 per annum remained).[79] General factors were also influencing the picture. Rival sources of provision were increasingly overtaking the various roles of the Church. Some alternatives came in old forms, like the local pubs, others, like the gramophone demonstrated at a village event in 1901, were new. At a formal institutional level, responsibility for schools was vested in the County Council as the Local Education Authority from 1902, and national government welfare provision, such as the first old age pensions in 1908, was increasing. Church involvement in education and welfare did not suddenly end, but it was increasingly secondary. The great abbey church was at once a glory and an enormous drain on local adherents, whose numbers seem to have become harder to maintain. In all of this, Poyntz's personality was an added factor, combining as it did conscientious service, confrontational conviction and perhaps deterrent judgements. His legacy after 1920 was a mixed one, the abbey still reflecting his High Church style but also reflecting longer-term trends in Dorchester and beyond, over which Poyntz had little influence.

Chapter Seven

Dorchester and its Abbey Recollected, 1920–2005

NICHOLAS DUDLEY

This is the first period of the abbey's history for which it has been possible to hear directly from some of the leading players. The testimony of people born in Dorchester and of clergy and residents who remember the events and attitudes of the time has been collected. Together with other sources this tells of very different times for the abbey before and after 1957.

Continuities and Decline, 1920–1957

Nathaniel Poyntz's thirty-four years as vicar were followed by two short incumbencies which signalled an intention to follow his High Church style. William Bartlett was vicar from 1920 to 1921, at the end of his career, and William Drake from 1922 to 1925, before his main ministry in Bedfordshire. Interestingly both had been curates at St John the Divine, Kennington, in south London, where Bartlet had also been vicar from 1917. St John's was one of the most ritualist churches in London, described by Mudie-Smith in his survey of London religion in 1902–3 as a vigorous community 'with its ten curates and its vast organisation'.

After their brief ministries, Dorchester returned to a pattern of long-staying and influential vicars, with the arrival of the Revd Henry George Lancaster. Born in 1863 and ordained in 1887, he married his first bishop's daughter, ministered in Suez, Beirut and Brussels and was for twenty-two years Vicar of Wybunbury (Cheshire), arriving in Dorchester in 1927 a much travelled man, already in his late sixties and with

forty years of his ministry behind him. Despite this he remained for over thirty years, dying in post aged 94 in 1957.

The first two years of Lancaster's ministry retained a grand style, with the Sung Eucharist at 8 am an impressive affair, celebrated by him at the People's Altar with three other priests officiating and a fine choir of thirty students from the Missionary College, in addition to the Dorchester men and boy choristers. In 1929 the College moved, with shrinking student numbers, to Burcot and its members could attend only Sunday services. Then, in 1940, it closed. Lancaster was on his own. Throughout the war years he celebrated Holy Communion each morning, although nearing his eightieth year. The abbey had to comply with 'blackout' restrictions and even the early morning candles on the People's Altar caused problems with the police and air raid wardens. The arrival of American aircrew based at Mount Farm and the large numbers of prisoners of war held in the locality extended his commitments, which included in the immediate post-war years a number of weddings between local women and Americans from the base and some Poles who had remained in Britain after their release.

The routine worship in the abbey after the war is recalled as austere and sombre, with fewer and fewer people in the congregation. Lancaster officiated at the high altar and hardly anyone could hear his increasingly frail voice. He continued to favour High Church practices and was frequently obscured from view by copious clouds of incense from a censer, swung constantly by one of four boy servers then routinely in attendance. Another server, the 'boat boy', carried fresh supplies to ensure no break in fumigation.

Two of those servers, then in their early teens, still live in the village. They remember the abbey as decidedly dilapidated, dirty and dingy, perhaps partly explained by the lighting (paraffin lamps at the end of each pew) and heating. At the west end of the abbey were two massive furnaces, fired by coke and requiring regular stoking. One of the stokers slaved away before services to generate the hot air that was then directed forward over the congregation. The smoke and fumes were fed back into an area under the tower, where a flue led to the outside. Archaeologists recorded the vestiges of this system in 2001. Not surprisingly the whole area, where the choir now robe, was appallingly grimy.

At the north-east end, the present vestry was linked with the nave. The organ stood at the present entrance to the St Birinus Chapel. The wooden choir screens were backed by red curtains, not to be replaced till after Lancaster's time. The choir eventually included females, their heads covered by blue veils. Black cassocks were worn for most services, with red ones for high days and holidays. Besides the daily offices, during term time the whole village school, both juniors and seniors, processed weekly from Queen Street to the abbey for worship.

Lancaster's personal life still excites comment from those who remember him. There seems to be an incontrovertible body of village opinion that he 'chased the girls'. His wife, Helen Fanny, was seen as formidable, holding the purse strings and having private wealth. This enabled her to donate half the cost of the building for a new village school. Together, Lancaster and his wife donated the vicarage orchard garden for the playground. When his wife died, in April 1932, Lancaster engaged a housekeeper, named Sarah,

60. *The Revd Henry Lancaster, vicar from 1927 to 1957*

who is said to have been rather neglectful in her care of him. Maybe this explains in part his reputation with the ladies. Reassuringly, in the words of the longest-living resident in the village, 'no harm was done'. The 'chase' was duly rewarded at the age of 69, when he married, as his second wife, the 37-year-old Phyllis Mary Baring, niece of his housekeeper. The wedding ceremony took place outside the village and is remembered as being reported in the *News of the World*. Lancaster died on 1 January 1957 and was buried in an impressive grave on raised ground, near the centre of the cemetery, alongside his first wife. Eventually they were joined by his second wife.

61. The reconstructed shrine to St Birinus, dedicated in 1964 in memory of Gerald Allen, first holder of the new suffragan bishopric of Dorchester, which was created in 1939. The roof of the shrine was removed in 2005.

Lancaster's era may be accounted a time of neglect and deterioration for the abbey, although his age, the unpopularity of some of his churchmanship, the great size of the abbey, and the size and wealth of the local population all need to be taken into consideration. It is rarely acknowledged that Lancaster was instrumental in launching a restoration fund for the abbey, which raised over £12,000 – a very considerable sum at the time, the bulk of the contributions being from small local donations.

When, on 26 June 1952, a thanksgiving service for the restoration was held in the abbey, it was attended by Dr G. B. Allen, the first Bishop of Dorchester since the eleventh century and the first holder of the new suffragan bishopric created in the Oxford diocese in 1939. (The Bishop of Dorchester is now one of three area bishops in the diocese, alongside those of Buckingham and Reading.) When, in 1964, a reconstruction of the shrine of St Birinus was dedicated in the abbey, it was in memory of Bishop Allen.

New Directions: Best, Nichols and others, 1957–1987

In 1957 the fortunes of the abbey changed with the arrival of the first of what was to be a series of younger, energetic clergymen. They were operating in a changing context – local and national, ecclesiastical and secular – and their successful response to it produced new purpose and new directions for the church in Dorchester.

The Revd Harold Best (vicar from 1957 to 1974) trained as an architect before ordination at the age of 32. He came to Dorchester with his architect wife and young family, full of ideas for the restoration of the abbey and keen to promote and enhance the profile and relevance of the building in the second half of the twentieth century. Best was 'low church' compared with his predecessors and soon moved the Eucharist during Matins from the high altar to an altar in the chancel. The priest now faced the people and was audible. Best also had the opportunity to create another new setting for worship. In 1960 a developing settlement, Berinsfield, was designated within the parish on the site of the former Mount Farm airfield. The Anglican church of St Mary and St Berin (1962) was designed by Harold Best, one of the earliest attempts to provide a new place, criticized for its dreary environment of council housing and social problems, with a community infrastructure.

Best is remembered for his gentle manner, hiding an iron determination, and 'a heavenly sense of humour, patience and tolerance'. These attributes helped him direct the not inconsiderable energies of some very strong-willed voluntary helpers, especially Edith Stedman, a feisty 'Yankee' (her words), who for seventeen years migrated to England for six months every summer after retirement in 1954 as Director of the Appointments Board at the Ivy League Radcliffe College in Boston. On her visits she stayed as a paying guest with Diana Macdonald, who eventually became the owner of Dorchester Manor. Soon the prime reason for Stedman's visits to England was 'the abbey', with which she had fallen head over heels in love. In due course she became an abbey guide. In 1958 she took up Harold Best's proposal to turn the run-down school vegetable plot into a cloister

63. *The Revd Harold Best, vicar from 1957 to 1974*

62. *A new church for a new settlement: St Mary and St Berin (built 1962) in Berinsfield*

garden. She planned a spacious lawn, landscaped beds and benches, where mothers could rest with their children, as an Anglo-American memorial garden, a gift from the people of America. It would be fun, she thought, to raise the equivalent sum of money (£140) as that originally paid by Richard Beauforest for the abbey in the 1540s. The precise modern equivalent sum was not revealed but it amounted to many thousands of dollars. Stedman's fullest powers of persuasion were needed, as she recorded with considerable humour in her booklet *A Yankee in an English Village*. Stedman's public persona was dominant but in her booklet, the role of others, notably successive secretary/ administrators of the American Friends of Dorchester Abbey, formed in the winter of 1957, is generously acknowledged.

Around the same time, Best initiated an English Association of Friends of the Abbey, which eventually absorbed many of the American friends and continues to support the abbey to the present day. Stedman was initially rather scathing about the genteel approach of the English Friends and thought their appeal 'wouldn't wring water out of a dishcloth'. Best was undeterred and the English Friends' appeal reached its total based largely on smaller-scale local effort.

In the summer of 1959 a festival for the Friends of the Abbey was held, with the ringing of changes and a solemn sung Eucharist attended by the Bishop of Oxford. The top brass of the USAF were invited to the rectory garden party afterwards, for once with perfect English sunshine. Stedman broached the subject of USAF tractors being volunteered to clear the area of the American garden. The lieutenant colonels did not jump to the challenge, but were eventually coerced through their wives. A year later the lawn had been sown, a spindly hedge was in place and memorial beeches were starting to show shoots. Money came from the States for six teak memorial benches, some of which still survive with their memorial inscriptions. Stedman persuaded the old Oxford firm of Coopers to give a 10% 'ecclesiastical discount'. A large oak cross in memory of all pre-Reformation donors to the abbey was dedicated by the Bishop of Buckingham and still stands on the east side of the garden. The garden was opened formally on 22 May 1960 with a Rogation procession, described as a 'rather homely affair'. Best, preceded by the crucifer and acolytes, was followed by the congregation, who sang the Litany.

In 1960 attention switched to the south of the church, with the preparation of the rose garden leading to the south door and essential repairs to the south wall of the People's Chapel, the subject of the separate appeal by the English

Friends for £30,000. In that year, too, Harold Best commissioned an opera, *The Jesse Tree*, directed by Daphne Marshall, to be premiered at the first abbey Festival of Drama and Music. Over the years the festival has brought many people into the abbey for the first time in their lives, fulfilling Best's wish that a wider public should appreciate spiritually uplifting music in the beauty of the abbey. The festival generated a regular income for maintenance. At the twenty-first festival in 1980, the drama moved to the village hall, marking the start of theatrical productions by the Dorchester Amateur Dramatic Society.

Stedman meanwhile turned her attention to the abbey guest house, probably built to accommodate pilgrims to the shrine of St Birinus. From 1651 to 1652 it was a grammar school, then a private boarding school, and from 1858 to 1891 the boys' National School. It then languished until Stedman conceived the idea of turning it into a museum, eventually with a gift shop to make it pay. She also had the idea of compiling an *Abbey Guest House Cook Book*, a joint project with the Roman Catholic Church of St Birinus. Recipes poured in from Roman Catholic and Anglican convents and monasteries at home and abroad, varying from a Trappist offering of a twenty-five pork chop concoction to 'Fou-Fou'/ Bishop's Delight, to a hot pot by the mother superior of an Anglican convent in Oxford. Stedman, supported in the compilation by Reg Read, persuaded Chon Day of the *New Yorker* to produce one of his cartoons for the front cover. The cook book had to be reprinted in thousands. Each year the Museum and Gift Shop increased its takings, the proceeds covering plumbing, heating, reroofing, painting and the building of two small parish offices in the guest house garden.

Stedman's final major project was to persuade the American Friends to restore the great east

*64. Queen Elizabeth The Queen
Mother visiting the abbey
in October 1971 to celebrate its
restoration*

window in memory of Sir Winston Churchill, whose American ancestry on his mother's side was a sure-fire winner. General Eisenhower contributed a generous cheque. Soon all the fourteenth-century stained glass was packed in straw and sent to Norwich for cleaning and releading. The window was rededicated on 16 October 1966, at a service attended by the Bishop of Oxford and the Christ Church choir. For the first time since the Reformation, heads of the great Roman Catholic orders processed with their Anglican counterparts.

A highlight of this period was the visit in October 1971 of Queen Elizabeth The Queen Mother to celebrate the English contribution towards restoration of the abbey. (Under the leadership of Dr Mary Woodhall, the English Friends had raised £30,000 over ten years.) The

Brownies formed a guard of honour, a bouquet was presented by the smallest child in the village school, and the great and good of the county, together with sundry bishops, American priests, a Greek archimandrite and the Abbot of Douai, were lined up for presentation. After the service, the Queen Mother went into the marquee in the Cloister Garden and, separated by a bank of flowers, was on view to 800 people, amongst them a substantial contingent of American Friends who had flown over specially. Stedman was privileged to take tea with Queen Elizabeth. It seems to have been one of the more memorable days in the abbey's long history.

Many of Best's major achievements are linked with the work of Edith Stedman. In all probability it was not the easiest of relationships, that of an irrepressible American spinster

65. Portrait corbel (right), near the west door, of Edith Stedman (left), most active and determined of supporters, and founder of the American Friends of Dorchester Abbey in 1957 (photo courtesy 'The Times')

with a seemingly bemused English parson. No reminiscence about these two great characters would be complete without recalling one of their last conversations. Sitting one day in the vicarage garden, Stedman suddenly challenged Best, saying 'Vicar, how do you think God and I are going to get along together?' There was an immediate and heartfelt response: 'I think you are both going to have to make some adjustments.' A characteristic gesture by Best was to replace an eroded corbel above the west door with her effigy. Stedman was thrilled, never quite getting over the fact that she had started work in a women's prison and ended up as a statue on a medieval abbey. Some years after her death she was also remembered by the American Friends, who restored the lych-gate in her memory.

Following the Best/Stedman 'double act' was a tough challenge, taken on by the Revd Ray Nichols, another mature ordinand (aged 32), who came to Dorchester after having worked in Kenya and for the SPCK (Society for the Promoting of Christian Knowledge), the oldest Anglican missionary society. He arrived in 1974 as the new priest-in-charge of Dorchester-on-Thames with Berinsfield, charged with creating a team ministry, which would include not only

Berinsfield but also Clifton Hampden, Drayton St Leonard, Newington, Stadhampton, and Chiselhampton, together with the benefice of Warborough. Later, Marsh Baldon and Toot Baldon, Culham, and Long and Little Wittenham were added. This was part of a national response to declining numbers 'taking the cloth'. After much negotiation, on 29 January 1978, the team rector and five team vicars were licensed and installed in Dorchester Abbey by the Bishop of Oxford.

A team very different from that drawn from the Missionary College in what now seemed another age proved key to the new ministry at Dorchester. From the outset Nichols had the assistance of two non-stipendiary clergy – a curate, Father Laurie Ounsted, and a deaconess, Edith Fyleman. Laurie Ounsted had worked with Best. After serving for many years as a lay reader whilst working for the Sun Life Insurance Company, he was accepted (aged 71) for ordination by Bishop Carpenter of Oxford and taken by the Principal of Cuddesdon (Robert Runcie, later Archbishop of Canterbury) for training. He subsequently served the abbey faithfully for fourteen years. A commemorative plaque, dedicated by the Archbishop of Canterbury and Ounsted's son-in law, the Bishop of Guildford, was placed in St Birinus Chapel after his death in May 1984.

Deaconess Edith Fyleman was a former teacher from Roedean, knowledgeable in theology. She settled in Dorchester and undertook social work on the new estate, for which she is credited with proposing the name 'Berinsfield'. She was an active member of the team ministry and also served as the secretary of the Movement for the Ordination of Women (MOW), which began campaigning nationally in the 1970s with ultimate success. From her research into the life of St Berin (Birinus), she conceived the idea, together with Ray Nichols, of starting a pilgrimage based on the saint's role in bringing

66. Deaconess Edith Fyleman, active in the abbey's team ministry in the 1970s and 1980s, seen on the annual interdenominational pilgrimage (which she founded) to the abbey

Christianity to Saxon England. Thus came into being the twelve-mile annual pilgrimage from Blewbury Hill (where Birinus had preached) to the abbey (which he founded), followed by a service centred on his shrine. The pilgrimage, enthusiastically coordinated with the Roman Catholic congregation, is followed by an evening barbeque in the grounds of the Roman Catholic presbytery. Around 800 people attended the first pilgrimage service, accompanied by a large Salvation Army band from Reading, a regular feature ever since. Traditionally the Bishop of Dorchester walks the whole distance, carrying his pastoral staff and joined by people of all ages from far and wide. Family dogs come too, often joining their owners in the abbey. On one occasion eight dogs were in the congregation, one of which, with its priest-owner, had to be removed because of bad behaviour.

During Ray Nichols' first years in Dorchester, the village news sheet (then published as the *Church News*) expanded, increasingly reporting and commenting vigorously on national and international affairs. Highly unwelcome local news came in September 1976, when several falls of two-inch thick Victorian lime-and-hair plaster hit the floor of the nave from the ceiling sixty feet above. The abbey had to be closed and a vast network of scaffolding, occupying the entire length and breadth of the building, erected. An Oxford contractor, used to conserving ancient college buildings, advised covering the entire area of decaying plaster with plasterboard, secured with beading on to the wooden beams. The internal walls were cleaned down and painted with masonry paint. In 2000 this work was to come under criticism; the paint had not allowed the stonework to breathe, and breakup of the surface had soon occurred; some of the ceiling cladding proved to contain unacceptable quantities of asbestos; and concrete in the roof gully had promoted the growth of dry rot in beams underneath. In 1976 an urgent survey of needs beyond the immediate repairs had revealed loose tower parapets, timber beams affected by dry rot and death-watch beetle, weak main trusses, inadequate rain-water gullies and considerable crumbling and spalling of the stonework. Around this time, thieves stripped the lead off the roof of St Birinus Chapel and vandals removed bronze candlesticks from the People's Chapel, a much loved replica of the Holy Mother and Child (originally from Barcelona Cathedral) and several safes for visitors' gifts. Ray

Nichols must have wondered what more could go wrong with the vast building with which he had been entrusted.

Then, as so often throughout the long history of the abbey, help emerged. The very day the abbey had to be closed, a solicitor's letter arrived with news that Bishop Allen (the first Bishop of Dorchester in the restored use of the title) had left £20,000 in his will. This, with later additional bequests from the family, was to be used for abbey preservation. The urgency of this was all too apparent; a Dorchester Abbey Preservation Trust was set up and a major national appeal launched. Only £2,000 remained in the fabric fund. An appeal office was set up in the rectory and a former finance director of Pressed Steel, Fred McMullen ('Mac'), a faithful member of the Roman Catholic congregation, was appointed appeal director. He was untiring in his efforts over the next year, maximizing and investing incoming funds. The final bill was over £¼ million. All of this was raised during Ray Nichols' time. Significant events included a 'treasure sale', backed by Sotheby's and Christie's. The night before the auction the vicar and appeal director slept in the abbey, a sword by their side, to protect against burglary all the gifts laid out ready for the sale. A special Choral Evensong was held on 30 September 1979, when the appeal finally closed, having raised the funds to complete the necessary repairs.

Also during the Nichols era the Willis organ was relocated and restored, its original tracker action having become so heavy that even the most resilient young organists found their endurance and strength taxed to the limit. On completion the organ was moved one bay to the west and raised on a gallery, also creating a new vestry. A more convenient entry to St Birinus Chapel, previously reached through a door in the choir screen close to the high altar, was made. The old oak panelling which had enclosed the former vestry created in Harold Best's time was moved to form the choir vestry at the west end of the nave, where it can still be seen. The whole undertaking involved the removal of the Victorian pulpit, which had only rarely been used. A modestly elevated reading desk was made by the local firm Hallidays from old stored oak screens and was donated by John Beveridge in memory of his parents.

Music had played a major role in the life of the abbey, but in Best's time, and later in that of organist Richard Goodhall, the choir had disbanded. Now there was a revival with the arrival of Richard Barnes, a former Westminster Abbey choirboy and choral scholar at King's College, Cambridge. The singing of anthems, motets and advanced sacred music became a regular feature during Communion, and worship in the abbey was enhanced enormously. Barnes's successor, John Simpson, assistant bursar at Radley College, continues to serve the abbey both as organist and choir master to the present day, supported by two highly competent reserve organists – Dr Edward Olleson, one-time conductor and musical director of the Oxford Bach Choir, of Merton College and the University Music Department; and Dr Charles Mould, of St Cross, a former Secretary to the Bodleian Library, an organist in bravura style and a builder of harpsichords. The annual Festival of Music and Drama had been in financial decline but now experienced a revival. Another regular musical event during the Nichols era was the annual concert given by the London Mozart Players, together with Oxford orchestras, choirs and solo performers.

Ray Nichols' ministry in Dorchester was characterized by an unprecedented 'entente' with the Roman Catholic community. Pope John Paul II had called for greater ecumenicalism and Father John Garvey responded warmly. He and Ray Nichols instituted a joint celebration of the Easter

Ceremonies on Holy Saturday, when the Easter Fire was kindled outside the west door of the abbey and the paschal candle was lit and carried though the abbey. Garvey attended team staff meetings and Bible studies and frequently prayed with the abbey congregation. Catholic confirmations were celebrated in the abbey and Ray Nichols was always invited to be present in the chancel, the first person to be approached for exchange of the peace. The peak of personal friendship between the two priests was probably their joint pilgrimage to Winchester in 1979. This marked the 1300th anniversary of the moving of the West Saxon bishopric from Dorchester to Winchester and started with a Eucharist in the abbey, attended by the Bishop of Winchester and seventy others from the Winchester Diocese. Then, accompanied by people from Dorchester of both denominations, the Winchester contingent, along with John Garvey and Ray Nichols, walked back to Winchester. They carried a processional cross, designed by a young Catholic artist from Reading and enclosed in a perspex box, along with a piece of masonry from the abbey. The cross now stands near the shrine of St Swithin in Winchester Cathedral. No doubt the two priests, John Garvey and Ray Nichols – on their week-long walk of pilgrimage, during which they daily celebrated a shared Eucharist – reflected on how much could be achieved if their two churches collaborated rather than competed.

In 1985, not long after the scaffolding had been finally cleared away from the west end of the nave, it became clear that urgent restoration of the eight bells was needed, at an estimated cost of £15,000. This meant lowering the bells, so 'strong men in the village' were summoned. Starting on 2 February 1987, it took three local men four days to bring the bells down, saving a considerable sum in labour costs. This gave a rare opportunity to study the ancient bells at close quarters. The oldest, the seventh, was cast in 1375 and the tenor in 1380, so by the time Columbus discovered America these two bells had been ringing in Dorchester for more than a hundred years. Three more bells joined them while William Shakespeare was writing his sonnets and another during the Civil War. The two youngest bells were cast in 1867, when the Revd William Macfarlane was vicar. Characteristically the village rallied round with a bewilderingly succession of fund-raising events. The bells were transported to the historic Whitechapel Bell Foundry for retuning, which involved shaving away metal on the inside. The tenor bell, weighed for the first time in 600 years, was 17 cwt. The bells were finally 'lifted' by more strong village men, commissioned by the Lincoln College ringers on 18 August 1987 and dedicated and hallowed in a traditional ceremony on 1 November.

In the final years of Ray Nichols' incumbency, Deaconess Edith Fyleman and Father Laurie Ounsted both died in post. The increasingly familiar pattern of non-stipendiary ministers continued with Ken Reeves, a schoolmaster who became a lay preacher at the abbey and was ordained in 1988, serving as deacon. Edith Stedman died in America in July 1989, still in touch with her beloved Dorchester through visits and correspondence. Her ashes were scattered in the Cloister Garden. Nichols' earlier missionary and publishing experience were recognized in his appointment as editor of the Oxford Diocesan Magazine and chairman of the Diocesan Overseas Committee. This resulted in Dorchester hosting 'Partners in Mission', with delegates from all over the diocese and overseas, gathered with the local bishops and other Anglican and ecumenical leaders in celebration of a nationwide campaign. It was a highly significant and moving occasion, when the abbey became the centre for a truly international event. Nichols was made a canon of Christ Church in 1984, with emeritus status on his retirement in

1987. His incumbency had seen the creation of a team ministry, the involvement of non-stipendiary and female clergy, the growth of Berinsfield, the annual pilgrimage, ecumenicalism, a flowering of music through organ, choir and annual festivals, and the abbey building once more needing restoration to save it from collapse and closure.

What more could be needed? In the event, many demands and opportunities were to arise, with the abbey requiring yet more major care and development in the final years of the millennium, and with new chances to further its ministry in changing ways. It fell to the next vicar, John Crowe (1987–2004), to identify and take forward this work, and it is to mark the successful completion of this latest of the abbey's many phases of physical and pastoral development that this book has been created.

Across the millennia, 1987–2005

John Crowe was brought up and educated in an Anglo-Catholic tradition, reading theology at Keble College, Oxford (the home of the Oxford Movement), from 1959 to 1962 and preparing for ordination, in 1964, at Lincoln Theological College. He shared involvement with third world issues with his wife, Una, whom he met when they jointly organized a Christian Aid week. It was to be the first of many interdenominational efforts by this formidable husband-and-wife team, she a Roman Catholic and he an Anglican. This past experience was of great value when they and their four children arrived in Dorchester in 1987, following eleven years as team rector and Dean of Leek in Staffordshire. When interviewed later by a national newspaper, Crowe was described as 'mildly eccentric in a rural clergyman sort of way' and has freely admitted to being rather disorganized. Compensating for this were his wisdom and ability to delegate well.

67. The Revd John Crowe, team rector and vicar from 1987 to 2004

In 1985 John Crowe was elected to the General Synod and so his new parish was to have a voice in the national Anglican assembly, where the great theological debates of the day were taking place. In his time these included the ordination of women, distribution of church income from wealthy to poorer parishes, remarriage of divorcees in church, and promotion of homosexual clerics to high office. He has reflected that over the years he became less dogmatic and more liberal. In recognizing the need for churches to be inclusive and more central in their worship, he accordingly set out to include both traditional and modern forms of worship and more informal services in Dorchester Abbey as part of his ministry from an early stage. He also promoted wider use of the abbey, both for worship on a diocesan and ecumenical scale – with a focus on the St Birinus shrine, emphasizing its significance as a place of pilgrimage – and also for community use for concerts, drama and the visual arts. The value of the abbey as an educational resource for visits by schools and adult groups was increasingly realized under his custodianship and the open-door policy has seen an estimated 10,000 visitors coming to the abbey each year, probably more than at any other time in the history of the building. In his view, only this greater accessibility to the abbey for so many people, for whatever reason, could justify the major programme of development that took the abbey into the new millennium – not just the restoration of the historic building.

An early challenge was the deplorable state of the upper storey of the guest house, not considered a priority by either the Parochial Church Council or the Abbey Preservation Trust. Crowe found himself isolated in his desire to restore the building. He obtained a priming grant to develop a scheme and subsequently attracted a major benefaction from Sir Nigel Broakes, of the Trafalgar Group of Companies, who, on the death of his mother, Nan Alford, in 1989, donated £100,000 in her memory. He insisted that ongoing use of the building should pay for its essential maintenance. The balance of £107,000 was raised from other trusts and individuals, and by 1992 the guest house had not only a preserved and renewed museum and tea room downstairs but also a splendid meeting room upstairs. The dark, depressing and dangerous set of rooms above had deterred users; now the space became a prime site for meetings, lectures, quiet days, parties, art exhibitions and a dressing room for visiting performers in the abbey.

The tea room has been associated with an amazing success story, owing much to the industry of a single woman, Lettice Godfrey. She came

to Dorchester in 'retirement' and in 1977 began to develop the tea room in the guest house parlour. It became the venue not only of a lunch club but of a highly rated watering-hole for visitors from far and wide, with a star rating from Egon Ronay. Opening every weekend from Easter to autumn and for four days a week in summer, dozens of home-made cakes and large numbers of voluntary helpers were soon needed. Lettice, cast in the same mould as Edith Stedman, proved highly persuasive. As a sideline, she made pots of marmalade – most years in batches of 300 – for sale in the tea room. Proceeds greatly benefited local charities led by

68. Lettice Godfrey, whose work for the village included establishing the renowned abbey tea room, receives her MBE from the Lord Lieutenant of Oxfordshire, Sir Ashley Ponsonby, in 1991

95

69. The new sundial on the south-west of the tower, made by David Harber, of Bix, and installed for the new millennium

the abbey and now, under her successor, Margot Metcalfe, regularly exceed £9,000 a year. Such dedicated service richly deserved the award of an MBE. Lettice Godfrey herself modestly feels there may have been some confusion and that the award is in reality the BEM medal for 'Best English Marmalade'.

In July 1989 John Crowe and Ken Reeves suggested establishing a link with Jouarre, the village near Meaux approximately 70 km east of Paris, from where Agilbert, the second Bishop of Dorchester came, and where, in the crypt of the abbey he founded, the tombs of him and his sister, Telchilde, the first abbess, survive. Village opinion on both sides of the Channel was enthusiastic and ever since, parties from Dorchester and Jouarre have visited their counterparts, alternating on a yearly basis. There is a strong religious component to the long weekends and great opportunities to enjoy each other's culture.

The music of the village has remained centred on the abbey. The annual music festival has continued. In 1999 John Lubbock started a new series of concerts entitled 'Music in the Abbey'. The famous orchestra of St John's, Smith Square, of which he is conductor and artistic director, has come for two weekends in early September each year.

The year 1999 also heralded possibly the most ambitious restoration and development campaign in the entire history of the abbey, making the last five years of John Crowe's ministry before his retirement amongst the busiest. In November 1998 he met a small campaign committee – Hugo Brunner, Lord Lieutenant of the County; Christopher Gibbs, philanthropist; the Revd John Rick III, a professional American fund-raiser and regular locum to the rector; and John Metcalfe, on the PCC and destined to become a highly efficient clerk of works – to discuss his plans for the abbey to undergo major changes to make it more inclusive and welcoming in the new millennium. The architect, Martin Ashley, identified a long list of priorities, starting with the familiar quest to warm 'God's frozen people', the heating installed during the 1980s having proved the latest to fail to make a significant impact. A separate 'pentice' building on the north side of the nave was proposed to house a high capacity gas-fired boiler and to provide toilet facilities and exhibition space. It would also accommodate the many pieces of medieval masonry then scattered around the building. The exterior was to be made more welcoming by floodlighting. This was installed later the same year. Low-level lights along the Rose Walk and along the paths to the entrance, together with the main lighting of the building, allowed the abbey's architectural beauty to be dramatically highlighted.

At the south-west porch a more 'user-friendly' entrance was proposed, to replace the dark, Victorian, box-like structure inside. Inside, the damp blistering masonry paint was an eyesore. Redecoration of all the walls was therefore another priority. There were also major concerns about the state of the nave roof, both inside and out. A more flexible seating arrangement than that provided by the old pews was also considered essential. Redesign of the sanctuary area and development of the west end of the abbey completed the formidable list of projects. An ambitious target of £5 million was set, including a substantial sum for investment, which it was hoped would generate income for the future upkeep of the abbey, avoiding the need for repeated further appeals.

This concentration on money and physical fabric prompted John Crowe to remind everyone of the primary need for the abbey to be the centre for people's spiritual needs. The response was never clearer than at the new millennium. Over 600 people, many in festive gear from earlier parties around Dorchester, crowded into the abbey as midnight approached. For weeks beforehand many people had signed their names and recorded hopes for the new millennium on stars made of card, which were suspended in the People's Chapel. All around the abbey hundreds of candles were placed or carried alongside the glasses of wine provided by the Parish Council. The bells rang in the year 2000, a hunting horn was sounded inside the abbey by the landlord of the Plough and then fireworks were heard and lit up the night sky outside. Two hundred people remained when the millennium resolution was recited, vowing to strive for a better world in the new century and millennium. The first day of January 2000 dawned a beautiful day, the noon-day sun cast a perfect shadow on the new sundial and the bells pealed out again for a special celebration service, including a 'Sound picture of Dorchester in 999 AD'.

The abbey campaign appeal was officially launched on 30 June 2000, with a special event in the abbey. All 410 seats were taken, and by mid-April 2001 the halfway target of £2.5 million had been reached, with sufficient financial security for

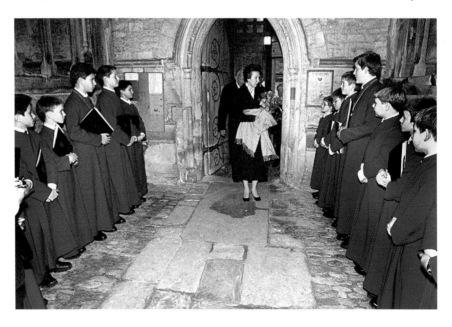

70. The Princess Royal attends a carol service at the abbey in aid of the Home Farm Trust in December 2001

Phase 1 to proceed. This focused on the 'pentice' and required excavating a large area in the Cloister Garden for foundations. The findings of the excavations are described by Graham Keevill in Chapter 2. The pentice was then built, magnificently constructed with an internal frame of green oak beams, braced and jointed with wooden dowels. The work was directed by Peter McCurry, previously involved with the reconstructed Globe Theatre in London. The pentice was roofed in Cotswold Stone. Inside the abbey, all the pews were removed and trenches dug, so that underfloor heating ducts could be

laid. An entirely new floor was put down in the shrine chapel area. All this work was completed by the spring of 2002.

September 2002 signalled Phase 2, with 350 tons of scaffolding erected to enable work on St Birinus Chapel and the nave roofs and ceilings to be done. Protective plywood boxes were built around gravestones, tombs and other vulnerable masonry. Asbestos dust left behind in the 1970s was collected. Over the next nine months, three-quarters of the nave roof was retiled. Damp had allowed dry rot and death-watch beetle infestation to become established and repairs were undertaken using resin and steel rods and plates, including repairs to two beams further affected in the shrine chapel, which could have resulted in a major ceiling collapse. Internal walls were stripped of plaster, revealing medieval wall paintings in the shrine chapel and Victorian wall-paintings below the string-course of the Lady Chapel. These may be further restored if funds permit. The old plaster was replaced with lime plaster and three coats of traditional limewash. A ground-probing radar survey (GPR) revealed numerous graves and vaults under the floor of the west end of the nave and People's Chapel.

At the other end of the building, work on the south-west entrance was delayed when the Victorian Society opposed replacing the existing wooden structure. Ancient procedures were invoked and a special hearing of the consistory court in the abbey on 31 August 2002 ruled in favour of replacement. A superb structure, designed by Peter Scott of Martin Ashley Architects and incorporating glass panels etched by local artist Jane Macdonald, was given the go-ahead. This has made the entrance lighter, more welcoming and more accessible for the disabled. Inside, the restored walls with their warm glow have also delighted the eye. Remaining stages of Phase 2 include a design for a stonework display

71. The new interior porch (2003) with etched glass panels by local artist Jane Macdonald

72. The silver altar cross, commissioned in 2004 to mark thirteen centuries of continuous worship on the abbey site and portraying the baptism of King Cynegils in 635

by Chris Hudson in the pentice and refurbishment of the sanctuary and chancel. Close observation and analysis of the building, including some features brought to light during the works, has been undertaken by the church archaeologist, Dr Warwick Rodwell, who has compiled a detailed report on his findings.

Once the major work was completed and internal scaffolding cleared away, the abbey began to host an increasing number of major events. By the end of 2004, the Abbey Preservation Trust Appeal had raised £3 million and it continues to work towards a target of £5 million. A silver altar cross was commissioned from the celebrated English silversmith Rod Kelly and the leading enameller Alan Mudd to mark John Crowe's

ministry in Dorchester and to celebrate thirteen centuries of continuous worship on the site of the abbey. It portrays the start of that history, the baptism of King Cynegils at Dorchester. On 16 March 2005 a new phase began with the institution by the Bishop of Dorchester of the Revd Sue Booys as team rector and first woman incumbent.

In almost fifty years since the arrival of Harold Best, and across millennia, the abbey building and the church's roles have changed and developed in many ways. An open-door policy has brought worshippers of many denominations, or none, and visitors from all parts of the world. In 2005, awareness of Dorchester's importance as 'a key to the history of England' and a place of pilgrimage is stronger than ever.

Chapter Eight

Building History: The Abbey Revisited

KATE TILLER

The abbey's 'history has been eventful and curious, and not easy to decipher: a whole literature has grown around it.' So wrote Francis Bond, who, in 1913, was the first student of this great church to approach it in a systematic way recognizable to modern church archaeologists and historians.[1] Since he wrote, the abbey has seen almost a century of further investigations and developments. The resulting knowledge and remaining mysteries of this complex building have been reflected in the earlier chapters covering its history at different periods. Here they are brought together to enable us to look afresh at the building today.

Dorchester Abbey incorporates fabric from at least nine building periods, as a phased ground-plan shows. If the identification of some of the earliest walling, particularly in the north nave wall, as belonging to the Anglo-Saxon and early Norman cathedrals rather than a new, post-1140 abbey is accepted, then there are two more phases. Finally, with the construction in 2001 of the pentice on the site of the south walk of the monastic cloister, a twelfth, twenty-first-century phase is added.

How all of this is revealed in today's building can best be seen by perambulating clockwise, first round the exterior of the church, and then round

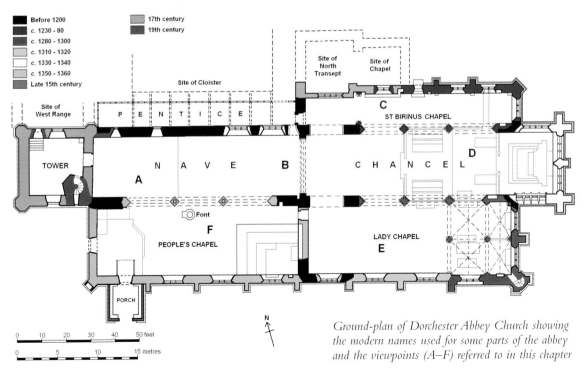

Ground-plan of Dorchester Abbey Church showing the modern names used for some parts of the abbey and the viewpoints (A–F) referred to in this chapter

the interior, looking at key features from a sequence of viewpoints. We start with that part of the abbey which incorporates the most extensive early fabric, the north wall of the nave.

THE EXTERIOR

I. From the **Cloister Garden**

- The tall, narrow proportions of the earliest surviving church, with its simple, unaisled, cruciform plan, unbuttressed walls and relatively small windows, are still apparent in the nave as seen from the north.

- The upper part of the wall has been dated to the late twelfth century, the early phase of the Augustinian abbey. The tall, round-headed window on the right was reopened in 1882. There were four such windows on the north and two on the south of the nave. To the left are two later windows with reticulated tracery, inserted in the fourteenth century.

- The lower part of the wall contains the earliest known masonry, now covered by the oak-framed pentice of 2001. Recent close interpretation of this stonework suggests fabric surviving from the late Anglo-Saxon and possibly early Norman cathedrals. The principal feature, at the east end of the nave wall, was a major arch, later blocked but thought to have led from the nave into a lateral chamber or transept of the Saxon cathedral. What is now the west wall of the north chancel aisle contains fragments of what would have been the east wall of this structure. The blocked arch was cut through by a fourteenth-century doorway, now linking the nave to the pentice.

- The grassed area is the site of the cloister created after the establishment of the abbey,

I

c. 1140. Unusually for monastic layouts, this lies to the north of the church. Some archaeological evidence and examples from other Augustinian houses suggest a possible plan of surrounding monastic buildings.

- In 2001 excavations in the area of the pentice uncovered successive Anglo-Saxon buildings of the fifth and sixth centuries onwards.

- The area lies between the line of the walls of the Roman town walls (to the right) and the River Thame (to the left). Scatters of Roman material have been found here, whilst a third-century Roman cremation burial was unearthed in the garden of the Revd William Macfarlane's new vicarage of 1857 (lying to the extreme right). It has been speculated that the area between that extramural burial area and the river might be the site of a temple similar to those found in some other Roman towns. More definite conclusions await further investigation.

- The Cloister Garden was one of the many projects to support the abbey undertaken by Edith Stedman in the 1950s and 60s. It replaced the school vegetable garden and contains a memorial cross to pre-Reformation donors to the abbey.

II. The **north chancel aisle** includes five phases of building.

- On the west (right of the picture) are the remains of the north transept of the original cruciform church. The outer half of the transept was demolished and the present spindly and crudely traceried window in 'Churchwarden Gothic' inserted in the early seventeenth century. The Romanesque doorway in the west wall may be seen from inside from the pentice.

- The first phases of the medieval aggrandisement took place in this part of the church. The transept was extended east, by the addition of two chapels in *c.*1220-50. The east end of this extension is marked by scarred masonry just to the right of the doorway below the central window. When the outer (or northern) chapel was demolished, along with the northern half of the transept, the late-thirteenth-century window (now seen to the right of the door) was repositioned there, one of several examples in the abbey of reuse of earlier architectural features.

- In *c.*1250-60 an additional aisle of three bays was added to the east and then (*c.*1270-80) heightened and linked internally to the chancel and to what remained of the transept. This created an aisle of five bays. The two windows on the left and the east window of the aisle date to this final, thirteenth-century building phase.

II

III. At the **north-east corner**, the eastward extension of *c.*1330-40, which forms the sanctuary, can be seen.

- The north window, with its flowing tracery representing the branches of the tree of Jesse, is in marked contrast in scale and style to the window to the right of it (the east window of the aisle), work of some forty to fifty years earlier.

- On the buttress just east of the Jesse window, is an empty niche, surrounded by late Norman, chevron ornament, seemingly anomalous amongst the fourteenth-century work. It is thought to be a late-twelfth-century feature, deliberately reset into the buttress.

- Walking to the left, around the east end of the abbey, one can appreciate the height and extent of the great east window, with its network of reticulated tracery and lack of mullions, and just how near the building was taken to the Thame and its flood-plain. Both contributed to the need to insert the substantial buttress which runs down the centre of the window.

II   IV

- The top of the window was blanked off by a lowered ceiling in the eighteenth and nineteenth centuries, and the present, traceried rose and the chancel roof are the work of Butterfield in the 1850s.

IV. At the **south-east corner**

- The south-east chapels (*c.*1280–1300) of the south chancel aisle crowd up to the sanctuary, which they predate by some thirty years. Their building took light from the high altar, probably a spur to lengthening the chancel.

- The turret staircase leads to an upper gallery and chapel, over two lower chapels separated by another substantial central buttress.

- Below the right-hand window is a good example of a 'barrow' door (temporary doorways used by builders and filled in when the work was completed).

- The south window of the sanctuary is another vast area of glass and variety of mid-fourteenth-century tracery, above which the distorted coursing of the masonry shows the stress the ambitious design put upon the structure.

- Below the south window niches were inserted for the trefoil windows behind each seat of the sedilia. These were the final features of the new sanctuary to be installed.

- This view from the south-east is that portrayed by Skelton in the 1820s, with the corner turret collapsing and vegetation sprouting from the stonework. In the 1870s the south chancel aisle and south-east chapel were restored by George Gilbert Scott.

- Nearby are the foundations of one of the cottages that encroached upon the edge of the churchyard in the post-Reformation period.

V. The **southern aspect** now presents a uniformity of fenestration and roofing which is misleading.

- The four eastern windows, separated by pinnacled buttresses, belong to the south chancel aisle, created in *c.*1310–20 to house the new shrine to St Birinus. The south-east chapels and adjoining arcade to the chancel were not long built, but it was important to open up a fitting area for the shrine. So the old transept, the new south-east chapels and the space between were united. Four matching windows were installed, with buttresses topped by carvings of men and beasts, mythical and otherwise. The contrast with the architecturally disunited and less grand north chancel aisle is marked.

- The wall beneath the windows is less uni-form, incorporating another 'barrow door' (below the second window from the right) and masonry probably from the Norman south transept wall (below the first window on the left). The width of the transept seems to have determined that of the new aisle.

- The churchyard contains an interesting range of tombstones, some alarmingly eroded and some as early as the mid-seventeenth century.

VI. The **rest of the south façade**

- The rhythm of windows and buttresses established to the east is maintained, but the building is slightly later (*c.*1350–60), and the details plainer.

- The nave of the church was already serving as a parish church and recent research suggests that this part of the abbey contained separate chapels and

V

provided a way to the shrine chapel to the east.

- Beneath its south-east corner is a crypt, an external opening to which can be seen low down in the wall. The crypt is vaulted, and partly above ground, seemingly more than a charnel house for depositing bones from the churchyard, as which it later came to be known.

- The porch is a later addition. Its outer arch is plain and late Perpendicular in style. Its floor is paved with stone, including a raised tomb

V

slab. To the right stands a medieval church-yard cross of limestone, much decayed, but most likely from the late fourteenth or fifteenth century. Whether this is in its original position is not recorded.

- In the same section of the churchyard are the tombstones of the Roman Catholic Davey family, who played such a leading role in Dorchester from the sixteenth to the twentieth century.

VII. The **tower and west end** bring together building from several periods of the abbey's history.

- The tower was rebuilt in 1602, perhaps because of the need after the Dissolution to remodel this area, where the abbey church was linked to former monastic buildings. Only the south-east turret was retained from the medieval tower. This is difficult to date, but is probably early fourteenth century.

- The Dorchester tower incorporates several potentially misleading features for architectural historians, long-and-short quoining (Saxon?) at the south-east angle; the plain round-headed windows on the second level (Norman?); and Y-shaped tracery on the top level (thirteenth-century?). In fact these do not seem to be reused elements, but part of an eclectic, seventeenth-century structure.

- The diagonal buttress with statue niches to the right of the west door of the church is of thirteenth-century design, and does seem to have been reset during the fourteenth-century building of this aisle. On its west side is the portrait corbel of Edith Stedman.

- On the south-west of the tower is the sundial commissioned from David Harber, of Bix, to mark the millennium.

VII

- In the belfry eight bells are hung; the seventh and the tenor date from 1375 and 1380 respectively, the sixth from 1591, the fourth from 1603, the fifth from 1606, the third from 1651, and the treble and second from 1867.

- To the left is the abbey guest house, its front façade incorporating a mixture of stone and brick. At the base are large blocks of ashlar, part of the wall of the abbey precinct. Behind this is a timber-framed structure, with a jettied corridor to the rear. This is consistent with a lodgings plan. An early-sixteenth-century date is suggested but full research is awaited.

- The guest house has housed successive schools and is now a meeting room, local museum and celebrated tea room.

- The eastern corner of the guest house incorporates fragments of the jambs of a gateway (probably the pedestrian gate arch at the side of the main gatehouse to the inner precinct of the abbey) and of an upper window.

- The path between the guest house and the tower leads on between the vicarage of 1857 to the left and the site of the west cloister range (now the Cloister Garden) to the right, along the line of the medieval route from the abbey to its precinct and farm buildings to the north.

THE INTERIOR

The exterior of the abbey provides a guide to its history, many of the features of which are mirrored inside the building. Added evidence in the interior comes from the wealth of furnishings, fittings, architectural details and decoration still surviving. Here some of these are highlighted.

The church is entered through an inner porch of glass engraved by a local artist, Jane Macdonald, and installed in 2002–3 as part of the millennium project.

- From a standpoint in **the nave** (marked A on the plan on p. 100) the high north wall gives an impression of the Norman plan. The second window from the west, reopened in the 1880s, contains memorial glass to William Macfarlane (vicar from 1856 to 1885), who carried through the restoration that so greatly influences the modern appearance of the church.

- Excavations in 2001 uncovered the location of the original doorway into the Norman nave, which was between the south-west corner and the first arch of the fourteenth-century south arcade.

- The magnificent lead font is the only surviving fitting from the twelfth-century church and is emblematic of the parochial duties undertaken by the Augustinians.

A High Victorian view of St Birinus, from the stained-glass window of 1887 in the nave, in memory of William Macfarlane, who was instrumental in restoring the abbey and making Dorchester a Tractarian parish

- Built into the west face of the first pier of the arcade is a carved stone bracket, showing five monks in woodland with a small naked figure, apparently holding a horn to his mouth. This has been interpreted as the devil awakening monks, an ironic note perhaps, given the abbey's known lapses in timekeeping by the fifteenth century.

- Through the door in the north-east corner of the nave the surviving Romanesque doorway of the north transept can be seen, now sheltered by the pentice constructed in 2001.

- At **the crossing** (B) the chancel arch marks the west side of the central space which linked nave, chancel and north and south transepts in the Norman cruciform plan. The arch is in Transitional style of *c.*1175. The nave and crossing are still linked by the stone string-course running midway along their north and south walls. The east end of the

string-course marks the position of the former east arch of the crossing, demolished
during the rebuilding of the east end of the
abbey church in the early fourteenth century.

- The plain arches to the north and south
  replaced earlier entrances to the transepts.
  Their date is much debated (see Chapters 3
  and 4).

- The organ was moved to its position in the
  north crossing arch in 1980–1 and placed on
  a gallery, with a new vestry beneath.

- In **the north chancel aisle** (C), now called
  St Birinus Chapel, the changes of plan during
  its late-thirteenth-century expansion are
  confirmed by the short wall-shafts, probably
  intended to support a lower, wooden vault
  but overtaken by the building of a loftier
  aisle, linked by an open arcade to the chancel.

- To the right of the door is the flue of a
  medieval oven for the preparation of
  communion wafers, and to the left a niche
  containing a fragment of the piscina of the
  demolished north transeptal chapel.

- By the altar are three aumbries, cupboards
  for keeping valuables. The doors are modern.

- High up, in the south-east angle of the roof,
  is part of the angle buttress of the Norman
  east end.

- In the east window the abbey's oldest stained
  glass, a roundel of c.1250 (formerly in the
  south sanctuary window), depicts St 'Bernius'
  being blessed before his mission to Britain.

- Amongst the memorials on the north wall is
  that to Laurie Ounsted (d. 1979), lay reader,
  then (in his 70s) priest and a pioneer of the
  mature ordinands, who became part of the
  abbey's ministerial teams in the late twentieth

The windows of the east end incorporate sculpture of the mid-14th century, including this depiction of the mocking of Christ in the great east window (© Oxfordshire County Council Photographic Archive)

century. Another memorial recalls Edith
Stedman, the American fund-raiser.

- In **the chancel** (D) the three great windows
  at the east end dominate.

- On the left, before the altar rails, is the brass to
  Abbot Richard Beauforest (d. 1510). His name
  and abbatial crosier also appear on the end of
  the nearby choir stalls. To the right, a Purbeck
  marble slab, with the indent of an arm grasping a crosier, commemorates Abbot John
  Sutton (d. 1349, the year of the first outbreak
  of bubonic plague in England), whilst a worn
  alabaster slab immediately to the south-west is
  inscribed to Abbot Roger Smith (d. 1518).

The Jesse Window, as engraved for Skelton's 'Antiquities of Oxfordshire' (1823)

- There are two piscinas, that near to the altar rails marking the position of the high altar before the eastwards extension of the sanctuary in *c.*1330–40.

- The brightly coloured tiles of Butterfield's scheme of the 1840s can still be seen behind the high altar and Scott's reredos of 1874. Various of Butterfield's furnishings (typically with trefoil motifs) survive, including pews and the pulpit of 1853.

- The **south chancel aisle** (E), now called the Lady Chapel, contained the medieval shrine of St Birinus and now houses the reconstructed shrine of 1964, incorporating

medieval fragments. This is dedicated to Bishop Allen, the first bishop of Dorchester in the new creation (of 1939). The aisle also has the abbey's main concentration of tombs, several moved from the chancel in the nineteenth century (see Fig. 36).

- The cross-legged knight, a particularly fine example of medieval sculpture, dates from the 1280s, and has been identified as William de Valence. It stands to the east of the shrine.

- An elaborate late Gothic tomb chest, surmounted by the alabaster effigy of Sir Hugh Segrave (d. 1387), is now positioned in the east bay of the chancel arcade.

- On the opposite, south wall of the aisle is the monument of John Stonor, Chief Justice of Common Pleas (d. 1354). His recumbent effigy is in legal dress.

- In the second bay of the chancel arcade is the monument of a Saxon bishop of Dorchester (Fig. 26). The tomb actually dates from *c.*1300, when the expanding abbey was keen to recall its former cathedral status.

- Tucked away to the west of Judge Stonor's tomb are the fragmentary remains of a brass, originally with three figures, of Margaret Beauforest (d. 1523) and her two husbands, William Tanner and Richard Beauforest. It was Beauforest who bought the monastic church after the Dissolution and saved it for the parish. It is an unobtrusive place for so key a figure in the church's history.

- In the south-east corner of the aisle an ingeniously, diagonally set doorway (linked to the piscina serving the SE chapel altar) leads to the stair turret up to the gallery. This was probably an upper chapel, which could later have served as a watching-loft for the shrine of St Birinus.

- This area of the church was much restored by Scott in the 1870s. The stone vault over the eastern chapels had been lost and he rebuilt it. The altar of the north-east chapel is a memorial to Bishop Samuel Wilberforce of Oxford (d. 1873). The retable came from the Dorchester Missionary College and is a memorial to five ex-students killed in the First World War. The walls of the chapel have fine Clayton and Bell wall-paintings of 1864. These are decaying, whilst other Victorian painting (such as that below the Jesse window) is obscured. It is hoped to restore these works.

A small doorway leads through what would have been the external wall of the shrine chapel into the last part of the church to be built, **the south aisle**, now called the People's Chapel (F).

- In the niche by the doorway is a replica of a seventh-century sculpture of Agilbert, second bishop of Dorchester (c.650). The original is in the village of Jouarre, in France (now twinned with Dorchester), where the abbey crypt contains Agilbert's tomb.

- The aisle has two focuses: one is the chapel on the south, now marked by the raised altar, built over the crypt and set against fourteenth-century wall-paintings including a crucifixion, with piscina and sedilia in the wall and window space adjoining; the other is centred to the left and above the chapel, and is believed to have been a gallery with another altar, set against the shallow niche in the east wall and containing more wall-paintings. Pilgrims would have passed under this on their way to the shrine.

- An interesting contrast can be seen between the work of the Victorian restorers, in the Godwin tile pavement on the dais, and the original medieval tiles beside the screen.

- These medieval fragments lie next to one of the most quoted of the abbey's inscriptions, that to Mrs Sarah Fletcher (d. 1799), who 'when Nerves were too delicately spun to bear the rude Shakes and Jostlings which we meet with in this Transitory World . . . died a Martyr to Excessive Sensibilty'. Nearby is the memorial to another victim of worldly upheavals, Michael Desvalpons, archdeacon of Dol, Brittany, a refugee from the French Revolution, who was sheltered by the Catholic Davey family at Overy in the parish and died in 1798.

The modest brass commemorating Richard Beauforest, who bought the abbey church after the Dissolution for £140 and gave it to the parish

The Clergy of Dorchester

Bishops (635–1072)

The West Saxon See

635–c.650	Birinus
650–660	Agilbert

The South Mercian See

c.660	Wine or Wini
?	Leutherius
c.673	Haeddi
c.678	Aetla

The East Mercian See

c869–c.897	Eahlheard
c.897–c.909	?Wigmund; ?Wilferth
c.909–c.920	Coenwulf
c.920–c.935	Wynsige
c.935–949	?Aethelwold
949–	Oscytel (Archbishop of York after 951–8)
c.958–c.965	Leofwine (also Bishop of Lindsey and Leicester)
?c.965–c.970	?Wulfric
c.970–c.977	Aelfnoth
c.977–1002	Aescwig
1002–1006	Aelfhelm
1006–1016	Eadnoth I
1016–1034	Aethelric
1034–1049	Eadnoth II
1050–1052	Ulf
1053–1067	Wulfwig
1067–1072	Remigius (transferred see to Lincoln, 1072)

Abbots (1146–1536)

fl. 1146–73	Alfred
fl. 1185–1210	Eustace
c.1215–c.1223	Roger
c.1223–?1236	Richard
?1236–1259	Richard of Worth
1259–1269	John of Warwick

1270–?	Walter of Peterborough
fl.1285–7	Thomas
?–1294	Ralph of Didcot
1294–1298	William of Rofford
1298–1304	Alexander of Waltham
1304–1333	John of Caversham
1333–1349	John of Sutton
1349–1380	Robert of Winchendon
1380–?	Robert of Cuddesdon
?–c1440	John of Winchester
c.1440–c.1444	John Clifton
c.1444–1455	Alan Bateson
1455–?	Thomas
fl.1509–10	Richard Beauforest
c.1512–1533	Roger Smith (also Suffragan Bishop of Lydda to c. 1520)
1533–1536	John March

Perpetual Curates and Vicars (1544–)

1544–1557	John Mathew
1557–1559	William Edlington
1559–1571	John Hubank
1571–1577	David Morgan
1577–1579	Robert Faringdon
1579–1584	– Roberts
1584–1588	David Morrice
1588–1591	Hammond Cox
1591–1620	John Wright
1620–1657	William Winchester
1657–1662	William Read
1662–1667	David Thomas
1667–1674	Stephen Goodwin
1674–1684	Thomas Tuer
1684–1690	John Zee
1690–1714	Philip Keene
1714–1718	Thomas Lancaster
1718–1742	Joseph Norton
1742–1751	Thomas Cony
1751–1759	Thomas Winchester
1759–1763	Edward Acton
1763–1765	Francis Zernoult

1765–1785	Robert Stevens
1785–1786	Edmund Goodenough
1786–1788	Henry Mason
1787–1838	James Roe
1838–1840	Richard Walker
1840–1841	James Hughes
1841–1850	John Cooper
1850–1856	William Addison
1856–1885	William Macfarlane
1886–1920	Nathaniel Poyntz
1921–1922	William Bartlett
1922–1926	William Drake
1927–1957	Henry Lancaster
1957–1974	Harold Best
1974–1987	Raymond Nichols
1987–2004	John Crowe
2005–	Susan Booys

Suffragan (Area) Bishops (1939–)

1939–1952	Gerald Burton Allen
1952–1957	Kenneth Riches (later Bishop of Lincoln)
1957–1972	David Goodwin Loveday
1972–1979	Peter Knight Walker
1979–1988	Conrad Meyer
1988–2000	Anthony Russell
2000–	Colin Fletcher

Notes

Abbreviations used in the Notes and Select Bibliography

BAR   British Archaeological Reports
Bodl.   Bodleian Library, University of Oxford
CBA   Council for British Archaeology
COS   Centre for Oxfordshire Studies, Oxfordshire County Libraries
OAHS   Oxfordshire Architectural and Historical Society

OHS   Oxford Historical Society
OA   Oxfordshire Archives
ORS   Oxfordshire Record Society
OUDCE Oxford University Department for Continuing Education
OUP   Oxford University Press
VCH   Victoria County History

CHAPTER ONE: INTRODUCTION

1. J. H. Parker, *The History of Dorchester, Oxfordshire* (1882), p. vii.
2. Parker, op. cit., p. ix.
3. See bibliography on p. 117.

CHAPTER TWO: THE ARCHAEOLOGY OF DORCHESTER

1. G. D. Keevill, 'Archaeological investigations in 2001 at the abbey church of St Peter and St Paul, Dorchester-on-Thames, Oxfordshire', *Oxoniensia*, vol. 68 (2003), pp. 313–62.
2. See G. Briggs, J. Cook and T. Rowley, *The Archaeology of the Oxford Region* (OUDCE, Oxford, 1986), for chapters and maps on the palaeolithic, neolithic, Bronze Age and Iron Age. J. Cook and T. Rowley (eds), *Dorchester through the Ages* (1985) has a good summary of the evidence for Dorchester during these periods (and subsequently). D. Benson and D. Miles, *The Upper Thames Valley: an Archaeological Survey of the River Gravels* (Oxford Archaeological Unit, Oxford, 1974), map 36, shows the evidence from aerial photographs taken up to the early 1970s.
3. M. Henig and P. Booth, *Roman Oxfordshire* (2000), pp. 2–4; see also fig. 2.1 for a map of Roman roads and settlements.
4. J. Cook and T. Rowley, op. cit., p. 28.
5. B. Durham and T. Rowley, 'A Cemetery Site at Queenford Mill, Dorchester', *Oxoniensia*, vol. 37 (1972), pp. 32–7. R. A. Chambers, 'The late and sub-Roman cemetery at Queenford Farm, Dorchester on Thames, Oxon', *Oxoniensia*, vol. 52 (1987), pp. 35–69.

6. For an excellent summary, see J. Blair, *Anglo-Saxon Oxfordshire* (1994), pp. 5–6.
7. See Henig and Booth, op.cit., pp. 58–63, but especially pp. 59–61.
8. C. J. K. Cunningham and J. W. Banks, 'Excavations at Dorchester Abbey, Oxon.', *Oxoniensia*, vol. 37 (1972), pp. 158–64.
9. W. Rodwell, 'The Abbey Church of St Peter and St Paul, Dorchester-on-Thames, Oxfordshire' (unpublished report, 2005).
10. R. Daniels, 'The Anglo-Saxon monastery at Church Close, Hartlepool, Cleveland', *Archaeological Journal 145* (1988), pp. 158–210; P. Rahtz, 'The building plan of the Anglo-Saxon monastery of Whitby Abbey', in D. Wilson (ed.), *The Archaeology of Anglo-Saxon England*, Cambridge (1976); P. Hill, *Whithorn and St Ninian: the Excavation of a Monastic Town, 1984–91*, The Whithorn Trust (1997).
11. N. Doggett, 'The Anglo-Saxon See and Cathedral of Dorchester-on-Thames: the evidence considered', in *Oxoniensia*, vol. 51 (1986), pp. 49–61.
12. The timbers could be post-medieval, associated with an episode of refacing that seems to have occurred, perhaps around 1600, when the tower was rebuilt.

CHAPTER THREE: CATHEDRAL AND ABBEY, 635–1536

1. Bede, *Ecclesiastical History of the English People* (Penguin edition, 1990), book III, chapter 7, p. 153.
2. J. Blair, *Anglo-Saxon Oxfordshire* (1994), p. 39.
3. ibid., p. 45.
4. J. Cook and T. Rowley (eds.), *Dorchester through the Ages*

(1985), p. 37; Blair, op. cit., pp. 58–9; W. Rodwell, 'The Abbey Church of St Peter and St Paul, Dorchester-on-Thames, Oxfordshire' (unpublished report, 2005), vol. 1, pp. 22–5.

5. Blair, loc.cit.

6. N. Doggett, 'The Anglo-Saxon See and Cathedral of Dorchester-on-Thames: the evidence reconsidered', in *Oxoniensia*, vol. 51 (1986), pp. 49–61.

7. N. Hamilton (ed.), William of Malmesbury, *Chronicles and Memorials of Great Britain and Ireland: De Gestis Pontificum Anglorum*, Lib. IV Rolls. Ser., p. 312.

8. L. Toulmin Smith (ed.), *Itinerary of John Leland* (1964 edn.), vol. 1, p. 117.

9. Rodwell, op. cit., vol. 1, p. 30; earlier accounts came to similar conclusions, see Cook and Rowley, op. cit., p. 48.

10. See Chapter 2.

11. Rodwell, op. cit., vol.1, p. 29.

12. ibid., vol.1, p. 27.

13. ibid., vol.1, p. 32.

14. J. C. Dickinson, *The Origins of the Austin Canons and their Introduction into England* (1950), pp. 80–1, 86n, 87; David Knowles and R. Neville Hadcock, *Medieval Religious Houses: England and Wales* (2nd edn, 1971).

15. VCH, *Oxfordshire*, vol. 7, p. 52.

16. *Taxatio Ecclesiastica Angliae et Walliae autoritate P. Nicholai IV circa AD 1291*, ed. J. Caley (Record Commissioners, 1802), pp. 30, 43–5, 191.

17. G. Zarnecki, *English Romanesque lead sculpture* (1957); F. Bond, *Fonts and Font Covers* (1908); A. C. Fryer, 'Leaden fonts', in *Archaeological Journal*, vol. 57, pp. 40–51.

18. Malcolm Thurlby, 'Minor cruciform churches in Norman England and Wales', in *Anglo-Norman Studies*, vol. 24 (2002), pp. 239 et seq.

19. Rodwell, op. cit., vol. 1, pp. 55–7.

20. Cal. Papal Letters, vol. 1, pp. 95, 103.

21. ibid.

22. P. J. Lankester, ' A Military Effigy in Dorchester Abbey, Oxon.', in *Oxoniensia*, vol. 52 (1987), pp. 145–72.

23. Rodwell, op. cit., vol. 1, p. 61.

24. R. M. T. Hill (ed.), The Rolls and Register of Bishop Oliver Sutton, 1280–1299, *Lincolnshire Record Society*, vol. 52 (1958), iv, memoranda 56–7.

25. J. R. Lumbey (ed.), *Polychronicon Ranulphi Highden*, Rolls Ser. VI, 4, n. 6, 41.

26. Tim Ayers, 'The Sanctuary of Dorchester Abbey, Oxfordshire: its Design and Iconography', unpublished MA dissertation, Courtauld Institute of Art, University of London (1991); Rodwell, op. cit., vol. 1, pp. 63–7.

27. Ayers, op. cit.

28. The developments of the 18th, 19th and 20th centuries and their impact on the east end of the abbey are described in Chapters 4, 5 and 6.

29. Ayers, op. cit.; Rodwell, op. cit., vol. 1, p. 66.

30. Rodwell, op. cit., vol. 1, p. 65–6.

31. Rodwell, op. cit., vol. 2, pp. 148–50.

32. Cook and Rowley, op. cit., pp. 45–8.

33. F. N. Davis (ed.), 'Parochial Collections made by Anthony Wood and Richard Rawlinson', pt. 2, *ORS*, vol. 4 (1922), pp. 114–15.

34. A. H. Thompson (ed.), Visitations of religious houses in the diocese of Lincoln, *Lincolnshire Record Society*, vol. 14 (1916), pp. 68–83, vol. 35 (1938–44), pp. 115–22. A description of the visitations is also given in VCH, *Oxfordshire*, vol. 2 (1907), pp. 89, 115.

CHAPTER FOUR: THE DISSOLUTION AND AFTER

1. *Deputy Keeper's Reps.*, vol. 7 [Acknowledgments of Royal Supremacy] (London, 1846), App. 2, 285; L[etters and] P[apers, Foreign & Domestic, of the Reign of Henry VIII], eds. J. S. Brewer, J. Gairdner & R. H. Brodie, 21 vols. (London, 1862–1932), vol. 7, no. 1347 (p. 511).

2. *Valor Ecclesiasticus*, eds. J. Caley and J. Hunter, 6 vols. (London, 1810–34), vol. 2, p. 170; M. D. Knowles and R. N. Hadcock, *Medieval Religious Houses* (1953), p. 136; LP, vol. 10, no. 1238 (p. 517).

3. VCH, *Oxfordshire*, vol. 2, pp. 89–90.

4. A. H. Thompson (ed.), Visitations in the Diocese of Lincoln, 1517–31, vol. 2, *Lincolnshire Record Society*, vol. 35, (1944), pp. 115–22. A description of the visitation is also given in VCH, *Oxfordshire*, vol. 2 (1907), pp. 89, 115.

5. *Faculty Office Registers*, 1534–49, ed. D. S. Chambers (Oxford, 1966), p. 79.

6. ibid., 48.

7. Knowles & Hadcock, op cit., pp. 148–9. *Deputy Keeper's Reps.*, vol. 8 [Catalogue of the Deeds of Surrender] (London, 1847), App. 2, p. 36.

8. *LP*, vol. 8, pt. 1, no. 1520 (p. 576).

9. F. N. Davis (ed.), 'Parochial Collections made by Anthony Wood and Richard Rawlinson', pt. 2, *ORS*, vol. 4 (1922), p. 121.

10. VCH, *Oxfordshire*, vol. 7 (1962), pp. 52–3.

11. N. Doggett, 'The Dispersal and Post-Dissolution Careers of the Hertfordshire Ex-Religious', *Herts. Past & Present* (forthcoming).

12. S. S. Pearce (ed.), The clergy of the Deaneries of Henley and Aston and of the Peculiar of Dorchester during the settlement of 1559 and afterwards, *Oxfordshire Archaeological Society* (1918), pp. 182–3.

13. *Valor Ecclesiasticus*, vol. 2, p. 170.

14. LP, vol. 19, pt.1, p. 496. The grant to Ashfield is reproduced in full in H. Addington, *Some Account of the Abbey Church of St Peter and St Paul, at Dorchester* (2nd edn. by W. C. Macfarlane, 1860), pp. 170–1.

15. Anon., 'The Shrine of St Birinus, Dorchester Abbey' (1964).

16. R. Graham (ed.), The Chantry Certificates and

Edwardian Inventories of Church Goods, *ORS,* vol. 1 (1919), p. 26.

17. ibid., pp. 101–2,119.

18.VCH, *Oxfordshire*, vol. 7, pp. 43, 54.

19. Anthony N. Shaw, 'Tregonwell, Sir John [*c.*1498–1565]', *Oxford Dictionary of National Biography* (Oxford, 2004).

20. LP, vol. 10, no.388 (p. 155).

21. LP, passim.

22. L. Toulmin Smith, *The Itinerary of John Leland,* vol. 1 (1964), p. 117.

23. Printed in Addington, op. cit., pp. 98–9.

24. N. Doggett, 'Patterns of Reuse, the Transformation of former monastic buildings in post-Dissolution Hertfordshire', 1540–1600, *BAR* 331 (2002), p. 63. Examples range in scale and location from Dunstable and Elstow (Bedfordshire), Waltham (Essex), Shrewsbury (Shropshire) Fotheringhay (Northamptonshire), Crowland (Lincolnshire), Wymondham and Binham (Norfolk) to Lancerscost (Cumberland), Malmesbury (Wiltshire), Worksop (Nottinghamshire) and Bolton (West Yorkshire).

25. ibid., pp. 23–4.

26. C. Platt, *The Abbeys and Priories of Medieval England* (1984), pp. 239–40.

27. N. Doggett, 'The Demolition and Conversion of former monastic buildings in post-Dissolution Hertfordshire', in G. Keevill, M. Aston and T. Hall (eds.), *Monastic Archaeology* (Oxford, 2001), p. 172.

28. J.H. Bettey, *Suppression of the Monasteries in the West Country* (Gloucester, 1989), pp. 127–8; Platt, loc. cit.

29. F. Hancock, *Dunster Church and Priory* (1905), pp. 8–11.

30. J. Holden, 'The fate of monastic churches in Cumbria: a consideration of the position at law', in *Monastic Studies*, ed. J. Loades (Bangor, 1990), p. 265.

31. See note 22.

32. Bodl., MS Top. Oxon. e.263, f.62.

33. J. E. Field, 'Abbot Beauforest of Dorchester', *Berks., Bucks. & Oxon. Archaeol. Jnl.*, vol. 15, (1909–10), pp. 61–2; W. Rodwell, 'The Abbey Church of St Peter and St Paul, Dorchester-on-Thames, Oxfordshire' (2005), vol. 2, p. 112.

34. Rodwell, op. cit., vol. 2, p. 129.

35. See VCH, *Oxfordshire*, vol. 4, p. 365, for the establishment of the diocese of Oxford.

36. See note 23.

37. Rodwell, op. cit., vol. 1, pp. 50–1.

38. Doggett, op. cit. (note 25), passim.

39. Wood's plan of the church is reproduced in A. Clark (ed.), 'Anthony Wood's Life & Times, vol. 1, 1632–63', *OHS*, vol. 19, (1891), opp. p. 225. Among later antiquaries who copied and adapted Wood's plan are Richard Gough and Henry Hinton.

40. Clark, op. cit., p. 224.

41.VCH, *Oxfordshire*, vol. 7, p. 59.

42. Clark, op. cit., p. 225.

43. C.E. Doble (ed.), Remarks & Collections of Thomas Hearne, vol. 3, *OHS*, vol. 13 (1889), p. 185.

44.VCH, *Oxfordshire*, vol. 7, p. 61.

45. ibid., p. 59.

46 ibid.

47. Bodl., Gough Maps 227, f.33, reproduced in VCH, *Oxfordshire*, vol. 7, opp. p. 58.

48. Davis, op. cit., (note 12), p. 118.

49. N. Doggett, 'The Anglo-Saxon see and cathedral of Dorchester-on-Thames: the evidence reconsidered', *Oxoniensia*, vol. 51 (1986), p. 59.

50. Bodl., Gough Maps 26, f.42v.

51.VCH, *Oxfordshire*, vol. 7, p. 59; OA, PAR 87/11/A1/1 (Brief Book 1739–60); PAR 87/2/A1/1 (Vestry Minute Book, f.122 of which has the annual accounts of church expenditure from 1741 to 1755).

52. Bodl., MS Top. Oxon. d.795, ff.210–11; MS. Top. Oxon. b.220, f.113.

53. OA, PAR 87/11/A1/1; PAR 87/4/F1/1–4 (Churchwardens' Papers).

54. Bodl., MS Top. Oxon. b.283, f.12; MS Top. Oxon. c.688, f.42; MS Top. Oxon. b.220, f.111.

CHAPTER FIVE: THE ABBEY RESTORED, C.1800–1920

1. OA, MS Oxf. Archd. Oxon. c159. Dorchester faculties 1767–1792.

2. COS, OCL I 1321.

3. J. Skelton, *The Antiquities of Oxfordshire*, from original drawings by F. McKenzie (1823).

4. Dr Nicholas Doggett has done extensive unpublished research on illustrative work at Dorchester between *c.*1790 and the 1820s by John Carter, the Bucklers, Winkles, Neale, Hinton, Cattermole and others. I am grateful to him and to Kate Tiller for suggestions for the early part of this chapter.

5. Bodl. MS Top. Oxon, b.283 f. 12.

6. Bodl. MS Top. Oxon. b.220 p. 255; see also VCH, *Oxfordshire*, vol. 7, p. 59.

7. The placing of the pews in 1807 is shown in Bodl, MS Top. Oxon. b.220, f. 111.

8. See p. 48.

9. Bodl., MS Top. Oxon. a.64, nos. 11–12; MS Top. Oxon b.42, ff. 123–4; MS Top. Oxon. c.352, ff. 29–36; British Library, Add MS 36372, ff. 249–58.

10. E. A. Freeman, 'On the Architecture of the Abbey Church of Dorchester' (1851), in J. H. Parker, *The History of Dorchester* (Oxford, 1882), pp. 85–6.

11. Bodl., MS Dep. c. 589, ff. 224, 226, 230–1; VCH, *Oxfordshire*, vol 7, pp. 52–61.

12. Bodl., MS Top. Oxon. c. 103, f. 383; MS Dep. c. 589, f. 214.

13. J. Skelton, *The Antiquities of Oxfordshire* (1823), p. 4n.

The rearranged glass went into the east and south windows; the Jesse window on the north side of the sanctuary remained unaltered.

14. P. A. Newton and J. Kerr, *The County of Oxford: a Catalogue of Medieval Stained Glass* (Oxford, 1979), pp. 77–88; T. Ayers, 'The Sanctuary of Dorchester Abbey, Oxfordshire: its Design and Iconography', unpublished MA dissertation, Courtauld Institute of Art, University of London (1991), pp. 48–76.

15. J. Skelton, op. cit., p. 8.

16. See p. 64.

17. H. A. Addington, *Some Account of the Abbey Church of St Peter and St Paul, Dorchester* (Oxford, 1845).

18. He had prepared a design for a church in Newfoundland: *Ecclesiologist*, vol. iv (1845), p. 219. He later carried out restoration work in the parish churches of Forest Hill (1847) and Towersey (1850–4): J. Sherwood, *A Guide to the Churches of Oxfordshire* (Oxford, 1989), pp. 82, 188.

19. W. Pantin, 'The Oxford Architectural and Historical Society 1839–1939', *Oxoniensia*, vol. 4 (1939), pp. 174–8.

20. Bodl., MS Dep d.540 (papers of the Oxford Architectural and Historical Society).

21. Freeman, in Parker, op. cit., pp. 86–7.

22. Bodl., MS Dep d.540. The only completely new work was the construction of new finials and four statues: Freeman, in Parker, op. cit., p. 86.

23. Oxford Architectural Society *Proceedings*, 3 Dec. 1845; Ayers, op. cit., p. 38 and n. 45.

24. Sherwood, op. cit., p. 69.

25. Bodl., MS Dep d.540

26. *Ecclesiologist*, vol. v (1846), pp. 161, 259. Harrison designed the church of St George, Gloucester Green, Oxford, in 1849.

27. Freeman, in Parker, op. cit., p. 87.

28. For church restoration in general, see C. Brooks and A. Saint, *The Victorian Church* (Manchester, 1995), esp. pp. 51–81, 151–72. For Webb, see J. M. Crook, *The Architect's Secret* (2003), pp. 35–83.

29. P. Thompson, *William Butterfield* (1971), p. 44.

30. Bodl., MS Dep d.540. White also worked at two well-known London churches: Benjamin Ferry's St Stephen, Rochester Row (1847–50) and Thomas Cundy's St Barnabas, Pimlico (1847–50): S. Bradley and N. Pevsner, *The Buildings of England, London 6: Westminster* (2003), pp. 683, 764. The builder was again John Castle of Oxford.

31. Bodl., MS Dep. c. 589, f. 286.

32. Freeman, in Parker, op. cit., p. 88. Butterfield's tracery and his allegedly excessive use of ballflower ornament was later criticized in the *Ecclesiologist*, vol. xv (1854), p. 146, but the architect rebutted the criticism in a letter of 2 May 1854 (ibid, pp. 180–1), pointing out that enough medieval stonework remained for him to make the restoration an accurate one, and that he could not have carried out the work any differently.

33. *Ecclesiologist*, vol. xv (1854), p. 146; Bodl., MS Dep c. 589, f. 336.

34. Thompson, op. cit., p. 462. The architect did not approve of the result.

35. Bodl., MS Dep d.540.

36. ibid.

37. *Ecclesiologist*, vol. vii (1847), pp. 145–6; Freeman, in Parker, op. cit, pp. 88–9.

38. *Builder*, vol. x (1852), pp. 141, 407; vol. xi (1853), p. 408.

39. OA, MS Oxford Diocesan papers c. 748, ff. 61v–62v (faculty dated 24 June 1851).

40. Bodl., MS Top. Oxon. c. 103, f. 383. For controversy over the re-pewing and appropriation of some sittings in 1853, see p. 66.

41. *Building News*, vol vi (1860), p. 418.

42. *Ecclesiologist*, vol xv (1854), pp. 145–6.

43. ibid, p. 146.

44. ibid, p. 180.

45. Thompson, op. cit., p. 479.

46. VCH, *Oxfordshire*, vol 7, p. 56.

47. Bodl., MS Top. Oxon. c. 103, ff. 384–5; W. C. Macfarlane, *A Short Account of Dorchester, Oxfordshire, Past and Present* (Oxford 1881). William Addison had already appealed to the Oxford Diocesan Church Building Society for £1,100 to build a new parsonage, and G .E. Street, the diocesan architect, reviewed the plans in 1853, but the money was presumably not forthcoming.

48. Oxford Architectural and Historical Society *Proceedings* N.S. iv (1882), p. 75; *Building News*, vol. vi (1860), p. 418. The writer said that Butterfield's designs were 'conceived more in the spirit of the original work [than Scott's]. It is a pity that he was superseded.'

49. G.G. Scott, *Personal and Professional Recollections* (1879), pp. 87–8.

50. Bodl., MS Top. Oxon. c. 103, f. 383; OA, MS Oxford Diocesan papers c. 1796/2; OA, PAR 87/14/A2/1. There is an unsigned and undated design for the roof in Bodl., MS Top. Oxon. a. 24, ff. 102–4.

51. OA, PAR 87/14/A2/1; OA, MS Oxford Diocesan papers c. 1796/2.

52. The nineteenth-century paintings have since been whitewashed. A small section on the south chancel wall was uncovered in 2004.

53. OA, MS Oxford Diocesan papers c. 1796/2.

54. Centre for Oxfordshire Studies, photographic collection 4020. The organ was subsequently removed to its present position in a gallery on the north side of the nave.

55. A letter from May dated 30 January 1867, in OA, MS Oxford Diocesan papers c. 1796/2, makes it clear that a gate had already been erected by another donor,

J. C. Latham, and that the present gate was designed as a 'protection' to it.

56. Oxford Architectural and Historical Society *Proceedings* N.S. iv (1882), p. 76.

57. The subjects of the lower level are the Baptism of Christ, the Transfiguration, the Agony in the Garden, the Deposition, the Resurrection and the Ascension. The glass in the top row of lights is clearly by a different hand, but I have been unable to find its date or designer.

58. OA, PAR 87/14/A2/1; OA, MS Oxford Diocesan papers c. 1796/2; Macfarlane, op. cit. It is not clear whether the pointed turret at the south-west corner of the south aisle was designed by him or by Scott.

59. OA, MS Oxford Diocesan papers c. 1796/2.

CHAPTER SIX: RELIGION AND COMMUNITY

1. See Kate Tiller, 'Shop Keeping in Seventeenth-Century Oxfordshire: William Brook of Dorchester,' *Oxoniensia*, vol. 62 (1997), especially pp. 274–5.

2. OA, Cal. Q. Sess.

3. VCH, *Oxfordshire*, vol. 7, p. 52; M. Beak, 'The management of poor relief: Dorchester 1827–35,' in *Oxfordshire Local History*, vol. 5 (1998), pp. 19–36.

4. VCH, *Oxfordshire*, vol. 7, p. 50.

5. E. J. Hobsbawn and G. Rude, *Captain Swing* (Penguin edn., 1973), p. 112, app. 3.

6. Arthur Young, *General View of the Agriculture of Oxfordshire*, e.g., pp. 158–9.

7. VCH, *Oxfordshire*, vol. 7, p. 50.

8. Diana McClatchey, *Oxfordshire Clergy 1777–1869* (1960), p. 65.

9. OA, *Oldfield's Index of Incumbents and Licensed Curates*; McClatchey, op. cit., chap. 6.

10. McClatchey, op. cit., p. 70.

11. VCH, *Oxfordshire*, vol. 7, p. 63.

12. OA, MS Oxf. Archd. Oxon. b81, Dorchester Visitation Book; O.A. MS Oxf. Archd. Oxon. c159, Dorchester Act and Visitation Book 1740–1836, including Dorchester Faculties 1767–1792.

13. OA, MS Oxf. Dioc. c652, 654, c655, c649.

14. OA, MS Oxf. Archd. Oxon. c159, ff. 55–58.

15. Leslie Wood, 'The Dorchester Peculiar 536–1837,' in *Oxfordshire Local History*, vol. 1, no 5 (1982), pp. 2–15.

16. OA, MS Oxf. Archd. Oxon. c160, ff. 265–76.

17. VCH, *Oxfordshire*, vol. 7, p. 63.

18. P. Riden (ed.), *Dorchester-on-Thames Grammar School* (Dorchester Archaeology and Local History Group 1976).

19. *Oxford Journal*, 17 January 1801.

20. See, e.g., Kate Tiller, 'A nineteenth-century village boarding school; the Garlick School at Ewelme,' in *Oxoniensia*, vol. 57 (1992).

21. Educ. Enq. Abstract, 1833. PP HC 1835, vol. 42, p. 745.

22. Select Committee on the Education of the Poor, Digest of Parochial Returns, 1818. PP HC 1819, vol. IX-B, p. 722.

23. Bodl. MSS d.d. Bertie c17.

24. VCH, *Oxfordshire*, vol. 7, p. 64.

25. OA, MS Top. Oxon. c103, f.384. In 1853 the parsonage was 'in ruins'.

26. H. W. Taunt, *Dorchester (Oxon.) and its Abbey Church* (1906), p. 19.

27. COS, L DOR 942.57, Henry J. Hannam, 'Reasons for not taking part in the appropriation of sittings in the lately restored church of Dorchester, Oxon' (1853).

28. See Kate Tiller (ed.), Church and chapel in Oxfordshire 1851: the returns of the census of religious worship, *ORS*, vol. 55 (1987), pp. xi–x/xi for a discussion of the census and the Oxfordshire returns.

29. E. P. Baker (ed.), Bishop Wilberforces's Visitation Returns for the Archdeaconry of Oxford 1854, *ORS*, vol. 35 (1954), pp. 49–50.

30. B. Stapleton, *A history of the post-Reformation Catholic Missions in Oxfordshire with an account of the families connected with them* (1906).

31. OA, MS Oxf. Archd. Oxon. c160, f. 318, letter from David Thomas of 12 November 1662, and response of Official of the Peculiar, 13 November 1662; Dorchester burial register, 13 November 1662.

32. Anne Whiteman (ed.), *The Compton Census of 1676* (British Academy 1986), p. 426; county List of Papists, July 1706, quoted by Stapleton, *History of Catholic Missions*, p. 245; Britwell Catholic Registers, 1769; OA MS Oxf. Dioc. c432, f. 45.

33. E. C. Davey, *Memoirs of an Oxfordshire Old Catholic Family and its connections from 1566 to 1897* (1897), pp. 67–8; Stapleton, op. cit., pp. 246–9.

34. ibid., Michael Gandy (comp.), *Catholic Missions and Registers 1700–1880*, vol. 2 (1993), pp. 33–7.

35. Davey, op. cit., p 68.

36. OA, MS Oxf. Archd. Oxon., c161, f. 57. Letter of 29 April 1673 from R. Copock of Warborough to the Official of the Dorchester Peculiar.

37. Stapleton, op. cit., p. 247.

38. Gandy, op. cit., vol. 2, p. 34.

39. Davey, op. cit.; Stapleton, op. cit.; Mona Macmillan, 'St Birinus Church' (unpublished note, Dorchester Museum).

40. The 1851 Census enumerator's returns for Dorchester show Father Robert Newsham living with his niece and companion May Newsham, a servant and just two scholars, boys aged 10 and 9.

41. Conveyances and Trust documents relating to the Primitive Methodist Chapel in Dorchester Museum. The original indenture of 15 July 1839 records the sale of the Bridge End site by Moses Cherrill, labourer, to

William Coozens, William Brown, Charles Swadling, Thomas Tredwell, William Amsbury and Robert Butcher of Dorchester and John Dance of Drayton St Leonard, all labourers.

42. ibid. Extension of the above in the names of Henry Eggleton, William Brown, Charles Bowden, James West, William Huggins, Stephen Neale and James White.

43. Baker, op. cit., vol. 35, pp. 49–50.

44. OA, Quarter Sessions, Bridge papers 71 (letter of 1847).

45. Bishop's Visitation Returns of 1857, OA MS. Oxf. Dioc. d 179.

46. VCH, *Oxfordshire*, vol. 7, p. 56.

47. Most recently and fully discussed by S. A. Skinner, *Tractarians and the 'Condition of England': The Social and Political Thought of the Oxford Movement* (2004), especially chap. 3, 'Low Politics: the Parish Unit,' pp. 139–87.

48. 1871 Census enumerator's returns for Dorchester.

49. Bishop's Visitation Returns of 1857, loc. cit.

50. ibid.

51. OA, MS dd par Dorchester. School register.

52. OA, MS Oxf. Dioc. b70. Newspaper correspondence.

53. OA, MS Oxf. Dioc. c332.

54. OA, MS Oxf. Dioc. c341.

55. Nigel Yates, *Anglican Ritualism in Victorian Britain 1830-1910* (1999), p. 402.

56. J. C. Waram (ed.), *The Tourist's Church Guide* (London, 1874).

57. Obituary of W. C. Macfarlane, in Bodl. G.A. Oxon. 8° 264.

58. G. W. Herring, 'Tractarianism to Ritualism: A study of some aspects of Tractarianism outside Oxford, from the time of Newman's conversion in 1845 until the first Ritual Communion of 1867,' Oxford D.Phil. thesis (1984), p. 43.

59. Yates, op. cit., p. 84.

60. A full account is provided by Mary Tame, *Dorchester Missionary College* (Dorchester, 1996).

61. OA, MS Oxf. Dioc. c332.

62. Robert Sefton, *William Seymour Blackstone (1809-1881): a Wallingford MP* (privately published, 2003).

63. *The Times*, 13 August 1880.

64. G. W. O. Addleshaw and F. Etchells, *The Architectural Setting of Anglican Worship* (1948), p. 200, identify three types of altar – mysterious, dramatic and ministerial. Dorchester clearly developed into the second of these in the third quarter of the nineteenth century as the high altar was elaborated and raised, and the view to it from the west increasingly opened up to the congregation, albeit with the clergy, choir and organ interceding (see Fig. 17).

65. *Dorchester Parish Magazine*, July 1901.

66. Crockford's Clerical Directory 1888: Yates, op. cit., passim.

67. OA, MS Oxf. Dioc. c377, f. 283.

68. Yates, op. cit., p. 292, quoting the report of the Royal Commission on Ecclesiastical Discipline (1906).

69. BPP (1906) vol. 33. Royal Commission on Ecclesiastical Discipline, pp. 522ff., Q6998–7039: followed by letter from the Revd N. C. S. Poyntz, 20 January 1905.

70. ibid., vol. 34, Appendix A to the Report of the Royal Commission on Ecclesiastical Discipline, pp.29–30. Response of the Bishop of Oxford.

71. OA, MS Oxf. Dioc. c371, f. 143.

72. *Dorchester Parish Magazine*, April 1901.

73. ibid., December 1901.

74. ibid., October 1901.

75. Figures taken from Bishop's Visitation Returns for 1857, 1866, 1875 and 1887 and the *Dorchester Parish Magazine* for 1901.

76. Dorchester Museum, Conveyances and Trust documents relating to the Primitive Methodist Chapel.

77. Conveyances and abstracts of title of the Baptist Chapel, 1878–1973. I owe this reference to Professor Malcolm Airs.

78. Sheridan Gilley, 'Father William Barry: Priest and novelist,' in *Recusant History*, vol. 24 (1999), pp. 523–51.

79. OA, MS Oxf. Dioc. Papers, c365.

CHAPTER SEVEN: DORCHESTER AND ITS ABBEY RECOLLECTED, 1920-2005

The *Dorchester Parish News*, formerly the *Church News*, has been published nearly every month since the 1970s, edited by successive vicars. Individuals, too numerous to mention by name, have written articles on contemporary themes and events. These have been the single most informative source for this chapter.

Also invaluable have been the books by Edith Stedman, *A Yankee in an English Village* (privately printed for Dorchester Abbey Museum, 1971) and *How it Happened* (1977), an account of the founding of Dorchester Abbey Museum.

Ray Nichols and John Crowe have kindly recorded personal reminiscences of their time at the abbey.

Mary Tame, the gifted local historian with a prodigious memory spanning more than fifty years in Dorchester, has been most helpful in unearthing numerous photographs and archives from the guest house museum, where she works tirelessly.

The recollections of Jane Welch, Jenny Nudds, Philip Greenaway, Brian Rogers and John Pratt have also been extremely valuable.

Biographical details of the clergy were obtained from *Crockfords Clerical Directory*. Thanks are extended to the staff of Oxfordshire County Library in Oxford for their help in locating reference material.

Select Bibliography

A select bibliography of printed items relating to Dorchester and its abbey. The principal accounts are asterisked (★).

H. Addington, *Some Account of the Abbey Church of St Peter and St Paul, at Dorchester, Oxfordshire* (Oxford, 1845). Reissued 1848 in *Memoirs of Gothic Churches*, Parker, Oxford.

★H. Addington and W. C. Macfarlane, *Some Account of the Abbey Church of St Peter and St Paul, at Dorchester, Oxfordshire*, Oxford, 1860/82. New edn. of Addington (1845), with additional notes; also publ. as an appendix to Parker (1882).

G. W. G. Allen, 'Marks seen from the Air in the Crops near Dorchester, Oxon.', *Oxoniensia*, vol. 3 (1938), pp. 169–71.

Anon. [St. J. Hope], 'Dorchester Abbey Church', *Archaeological Journal*, vol. 67 (1910), pp. 333–5.

Anon., *A Short History and Brief Description of Dorchester Abbey, Oxfordshire*, privately printed, n. d. [1925].

Anon., *The Shrine of St Birinus, Dorchester Abbey*, privately printed (Abingdon, 1964).

M. Aston, 'The Roman Town Defences at Dorchester, Oxon; An Interim Assessment', *CBA Group 9 Newsletter*, no. 4 (1974), pp. 3–4.

R. J. C. Atkinson, C. M. Piggott and N. K. Sanders, *Excavations at Dorchester, Oxon.: First Report* (Ashmolean Museum, Oxford, 1951).

T. Ayers, 'The Sanctuary of Dorchester Abbey, Oxfordshire: its Design and Iconography', unpublished MA dissertation (Courtauld Institute of Art, University of London, 1991).

E. P. Baker (ed.), Bishop Wilberforce's Visitation Returns for the Archdeaconry of Oxford 1854, *ORS*, vol. 35 (1954).

T. Barns, 'Dorchester in British and Roman Times', *Proceedings of OAHS*, new ser. vol. 4 (1881), pp. 33–4.

M. Beak, 'The management of poor relief: Dorchester 1827–35', *Oxfordshire Local History*, vol. 5 (1998), pp. 19–36.

D. Benson and D. Miles, *The Upper Thames Valley: An Archaeological Survey of the River Gravels* (Oxford Archaeological Unit, survey no. 2, 1974).

J. Bertram, *A Catalogue of Medieval Inscriptions in the Abbey Church of Dorchester, Oxfordshire*, privately printed (Oxford, 2000).

J. Bertram, 'Medieval Inscriptions in Oxfordshire', *Oxoniensia*, vol. 68 (2003), pp. 27–53.

H. Best, *A Pilgrimage to Dorchester Abbey: A Guide to the Ecclesiastical and Architectural History*, privately printed (1967, new edn. 1969).

H. Best, *The Abbey Church of St Peter and St Paul, Dorchester, Oxon.: A Guide to the Ecclesiastical and Architectural History* (St Ives, 1970). [guidebook]

J. Blair, *Anglo-Saxon Oxfordshire* (Stroud, 1994).

J. Blair, *The Church in Anglo-Saxon Society* (Oxford, OUP, 2005).

R. Bloxham, *Dorchester Abbey, Oxfordshire* (Watford, 1990, and Dorchester, 2002). [guidebooks]

F. Bond, *Fonts and Font Covers*, Oxford (OUP, 1908).

★F. Bond, *An Introduction to English Church Architecture*, Oxford (OUP, 1913), pp. 254–69.

G. Briggs, J. Cook and T. Rowley, *The Archaeology of the Oxford Region* (OUDCE, 1986).

R. A. Chambers, 'The late and sub-Roman cemetery at Queenford Farm, Dorchester on Thames, Oxon', *Oxoniensia*, vol. 52 (1987), pp. 35–69.

W. A. Church, *Patterns of Inlaid Tiles from Churches in the Diocese of Oxford* (London, 1845).

A. Clark (ed.), The Life and Times of Anthony Wood, Antiquary, of Oxford, 1632–1695, described by Himself, vol 1, 1632–3, *OHS*, vol. 19 (1891).

★J. Cook, and T. Rowley (eds.), *Dorchester through the Ages* (OUDCE, 1985).

O. G. S. Crawford, 'Air Photographs near Dorchester', *Antiquity*, vol. 1 (1927), pp. 469–74.

C. J. K. Cunningham and J. W. Banks, 'Excavations at Dorchester Abbey, Oxon.', *Oxoniensia*, vol. 37 (1972), pp. 158–64.

E. C. Davey, *Memoirs of an Oxfordshire Old Catholic Family and its connections from 1566 to 1897* (1897).

F. N. Davis (ed.), Parochial Collections made by Anthony Wood and Richard Rawlinson, pt. 2, *ORS*, vol. 4 (1922).

T. M. Dickinson, *Cuddesdon and Dorchester-on-Thames: Two Early Saxon 'Princely' Sites in Wessex*, *BAR*, vol. 1 (Oxford, 1974).

C. E. Doble (ed.), Remarks and Collections of Thomas Hearne, vol. 3, *OHS*, vol. 13 (1889).

N. Doggett, 'The Anglo-Saxon See and Cathedral of Dorchester-on-Thames: the evidence reconsidered', *Oxoniensia*, vol. 51 (1986), pp. 49–61.

B. Durham, and T. Rowley, 'A Cemetery Site at Queensford Mill, Dorchester', *Oxoniensia*, vol. 37 (1972), pp. 32–7.

J. T. Evans, *The Church Plate of Oxfordshire* (Oxford, 1928).

J. E. Field, 'Abbot Beauforest of Dorchester', *Berks, Bucks and Oxon. Archaeological Journal*, vol. 15 (1909), pp. 61–2.

E. A. Freeman, *The Origin and Development of Window Tracery in England* (Oxford, 1851).

E. A. Freeman, 'On the Architecture of the Abbey Church of Dorchester', *Archaeological Journal*, vol. 9 (1852), pp. 158–69, 262–80, 329–35. Republished in Parker (1882).

S. S. Frere, 'Excavations at Dorchester-on-Thames, 1962', *Archaeological Journal*, vol. 119 (1962), pp. 114–49.

S. S. Frere, 'Excavations at Dorchester-on-Thames, 1963', *Archaeological Journal*, vol. 141 (1984), pp. 91–174.

A. C. Fryer, 1900, 'Leaden Fonts', *Archaeological Journal*, vol. 57 (1900), pp. 40–51.

M. Gandy (comp.), *Catholic Missions and Registers 1700–1880*, vol. 2 (1993).

M. Gelling, *The Place-Names of Oxfordshire*, English Place-Names Society, vol. 23, Cambridge, 1953.

S. Gilley, 'Father William Barry: Priest and novelist', *Recusant History*, vol. 24 (1999), pp. 523–51.

R. Graham (ed.), The Chantry Certificates and the Edwardian Inventories of Church Goods, *ORS*, vol. 1 (1919).

M. Harman, G. Lambrick, D. Miles and T. Rowley, 'Roman Burials around Dorchester-on-Thames', *Oxoniensia*, vol. 43 (1978), pp. 1–16.

M. Henig and P. Booth, *Roman Oxfordshire* (Stroud, 2000).

R. M. T. Hill (ed.), The Rolls and Register of Bishop Oliver Sutton, 1280–1299, *Lincolnshire Record Society*, vol. 52 (1958).

A. H. A. Hogg and C. E. Stevens, 'The Defences of Roman Dorchester', *Oxoniensia*, vol. 2 (1937), pp. 41–73.

F. E. Howard, 'Screens and Rood-Lofts in the Parish Churches of Oxfordshire', *Archaeological Journal*, vol. 67 (1910), pp. 151–201.

P. Jessel and E. Stedman, *'These Notable Things': 800 Years of Dorchester Abbey*, privately printed, n. d. [1970].

G. D. Keevill, 'Archaeological Investigations in 2001 at the Abbey Church of St Peter and St Paul, Dorchester-on-Thames, Oxfordshire', *Oxoniensia*, vol. 68 (2003), pp. 313–62.

J. R. Kirk and E. T. Leeds, 'Three Early Saxon Graves from Dorchester, Oxon.', *Oxoniensia*, vol. 17/18 (1952–3), pp. 63–76.

E. A. G. Lambourn, *The Armorial Glass of the Oxford Diocese, 1250–1850* (Oxford, OUP, 1949).

A. Lane-Fox [Gen. Pitt-Rivers], 'On the Threatened Destruction of the British Earthworks near Dorchester', *Journal Ethnological Society of London*, new ser. vol. 2 (1870), pp. 412–15.

P. J. Lankester, 'A Military Effigy in Dorchester Abbey, Oxon.', *Oxoniensia*, vol. 52 (1987), pp. 145–72.

E. T. Long, 'Medieval Wall Paintings in Oxfordshire Churches', *Oxoniensia*, vol. 37 (1972), pp. 86–108.

D. McClatchey, *Oxfordshire Clergy 1777–1869* (1960).

W. C. Macfarlane, *A Short Account of Dorchester, Oxfordshire, Past and Present*, Oxford, 1881; other edns, 1884, 1892; also published in Parker (1882), pp. 13–30.

B. J. Marples, 'The Medieval Crosses of Oxfordshire', *Oxoniensia,* vol. 38 (1973), pp. 299–311.

J. May, 'Romano-British and Saxon Sites near Dorchester-on-Thames, Oxfordshire', *Oxoniensia,* vol. 42 (1977), pp. 42–79.

D. Miles, 'Iron Age and Roman Dorchester', *Archaeological Journal*, vol. 135 (1978), pp. 288–9.

P. A. Newton and J. Kerr, *The County of Oxford: A Catalogue of Medieval Stained Glass.* Corpus Vitrearum Medii Aevi, British Academy (Oxford, OUP, 1979), pp. 77–88.

W. Pantin, 'The Oxford Architectural and Historical Society 1839–1939', *Oxoniensia,* vol. 4 (1939), pp. 174–8.

J. H. Parker, *Dorchester Church* (1845).

J. H. Parker, 'On the Roman Occupation of Dorchester', *Proceedings of OAHS*, new ser. vol. 2 (1868), pp. 90–9.

J. H. Parker, *A B C of Gothic Architecture* (London, 1st edn., 1881; 13th edn., 1907).

★J. H. Parker, *The History of Dorchester, Oxfordshire* (London, 1882).

★R. W. Paul, 'The Abbeys of Great Britain, No. 32: Dorchester Abbey', *The Builder* 78 (6 January 1900), pp. 11–14.

S. S. Pearce (ed.), The clergy of the Deaneries of Henley and Aston and of the Peculiar of Dorchester during the settlement of 1559 and afterwards, *Oxfordshire Archaeological Society* (1918), pp. 182–3.

G. D. Perks and P. O'Connell, 'Transcriptions of Gravestones in Dorchester Abbey Church, Oxon', unpublished MS in the possession of Dorchester P.C.C. (1996).

S. A. Peyton (ed.), The Churchwardens' Presentments in the Oxfordshire Peculiars of Dorchester, Thame and Banbury, *ORS,* vol. 10 (Oxford, 1928).

N. C. S. Poyntz, 'Notes on the Abbey Church of Dorchester, Oxon.', *Journal of the British Archaeological Association,* vol. 47 (1891), pp. 222–4.

P. Riden (ed.), *Dorchester-on-Thames Grammar School*, privately printed (Dorchester, 1976).

H. V. M. Roberts, 'Dorchester on Thames, Oxfordshire', *The Builder* 139 (5 Sept. 1930), pp. 378–9.

K. A. Rodwell (ed.), *Historic Towns in Oxfordshire: A Survey of the New County*, Oxford Archaeological Unit, survey no. 3, 1975.

W. J. Rodwell, *The Archaeology of the English Church* (London, 2nd edn., 1989; 3rd edn., 2005).

★W. Rodwell, *The Abbey Church of St Peter and St Paul, Dorchester-on-Thames, Oxfordshire: an archaeological and historical survey, with notes on the fabric and fittings of the church*, unpublished report (2005).

T. Rowley, 'Early Saxon Settlements in Dorchester-on-Thames', in T. Rowley (ed.), *Anglo-Saxon Settlement and Landscape*, BAR, vol. 6 (1974), pp. 42–50.

T. Rowley, 'The Roman Towns of Oxfordshire', in W. Rodwell and T. Rowley (eds.), *The 'Small Towns' of Roman Britain*, BAR, vol. 15 (1975), pp. 115–24.

T. Rowley and L. Brown, 'Excavations at Beech House Hotel, Dorchester-on-Thames, 1972', *Oxoniensia,* vol. 46 (1981), pp. 1–61.

F. Sharpe, *The Church Bells of Oxfordshire*, vol. 2, *ORS,* vol. 30 (1950).

J. Sherwood and N. Pevsner, *Buildings of England: Oxfordshire* (Harmondsworth, 1974), pp. 576–83.

J. Skelton, *Antiquities of Oxfordshire: Dorchester Hundred* (Oxford, 1823).

B. Stapleton, *A history of the post-reformation Catholic Missions in Oxfordshire with an account of the families connected with them* (1906).

E. G. Stedman, *A Yankee in an English Village*, privately printed for Dorchester Abbey Museum (1971).

C. E. Stevens and G. S. Keeney, 'Ramparts of Dorchester', *Antiquity,* vol. 9 (1935), pp. 217–19.

J. Stevens [W. Dugdale], *The History of the Ancient Abbeys, Monasteries, Hospitals, Cathedral and Collegiate Churches*, vol. 2 (London, 1723).

M. Tame, *Dorchester Missionary College* (Dorchester, 1996).

H. W. Taunt, *Dorchester (Oxon.) and its Abbey Church* (Taunt & Co., Oxford, 1906).

J. Teigh, 'Cathedral City that became a Village' and

'Splendour of an Ancient Abbey', *Country Life*, July 1963, pp. 1304–6 and 1410–14.

A. H. Thompson (ed.), Visitations of religious houses in the diocese of Lincoln, *Lincolnshire Record Society*, vol. 14 (1916).

A. H. Thompson (ed.), Visitations in the diocese of Lincoln 1517–31, *Lincolnshire Record Society*, vol. 35 (1944).

M. Thurlby, 'Minor cruciform churches in Norman England and Wales', in *Anglo-Norman Studies*, vol. 24 (2002).

K. Tiller (ed.), Church and chapel in Oxfordshire 1851: the returns of the census of religious worship, *ORS*, vol. 55 (1987).

K. Tiller, 'Shop keeping in Seventeenth-Century Oxfordshire: William Brook of Dorchester', *Oxoniensia*, vol. 62 (1997), pp. 269–86.

VCH, *Oxfordshire*, vol. 2 [ed. W. Page] (London, 1907).

VCH, *Oxfordshire*, vol. 1 [ed. L. F. Saltzman] (London, 1939).

★VCH, *Oxfordshire: Dorchester and Thame Hundreds*, vol. 7 [ed. M. D. Lobel] (Oxford, OUP, 1962), pp. 39–64.

L. Wood, 'The Dorchester Peculiar, 1536–1837', *Oxfordshire Local History*, vol. 1 (5), pp. 2–15.

N. Yates, *Anglican Ritualism in Victorian Britain 1830–1910* (Oxford, OUP, 1999).

Index

Page numbers followed by *illus.* refer to illustrations or their captions

Detail from the east window